THE DEEPER CENTRE

Roots hold a great mystery. Their ways are not known to us. If we try to expose them to the view of all curious passers-by, it is the end of the tree. So roots have to be hidden beneath the earth. They travel great distances in search of water and nutrients. We cannot control them from outside without endangering the health of the tree. We may prune and define the shape of the branches according to our imagination and cultural tastes. But we cannot cut down or limit the freedom of the roots. They sustain the tree in silence and freedom.[1]

THE
DEEPER
CENTRE

EVA HEYMANN

Foreword by Michael Ford

DARTON·LONGMAN+TODD

271. 9

First published in 2006 by
Darton, Longman and Todd Ltd
1 Spencer Court
140–142 Wandsworth High Street
London SW18 4JJ

ISBN 10:   0-232-52628-1
ISBN 13:   978-0-232-52628-8

A catalogue record for this book is available from
the British Library.

Designed and produced by Sandie Boccacci
Using QuarkXPress on an Apple PowerMac
Phototypeset in 12/15pt Apollo
Printed and bound in Great Britain by
Page Bros, Norwich, Norfolk

To Michael Ford
And to my sister, Lotte

CONTENTS

ACKNOWLEDGEMENTS

THIS BOOK WOULD NOT have seen the light of day without the help of many different people.

First and foremost I want to thank Brendan Walsh, editorial director at Darton, Longman and Todd; Michael Ford, author and BBC broadcaster, and my sister Lotte. Their support and encouragement has been a life-giving experience. They have taught me to trust that the seemingly impossible can become a reality: the finished book will be an ongoing sign that this is so. Their optimism was infectious. Both Michael and Lotte, to whom this book is dedicated, have been more than generous with the time they have given me.

I also want to thank David Walley, who was on call when needed – even at unusual hours. He enabled me to become computer literate, albeit at a basic level!

I thank my community for their support and Helen Forshaw SHCJ, who checked the references to Cornelia Connelly, our foundress. I am also grateful to Chantal Debreuil, who allowed me to refer to our conversation about prayer and meditation, and to Clive, who gave me permission to write about our retreat sessions.

I would like to express my special thanks for the friendship of Dr. Ilse Seibold and Frau Elfriede Schemel and their families. I remember with deep affection, Fritz, Elfriede's husband who died in 1993. These friends have not been involved in the writing of this book, but throughout many years they have been exceptionally supportive in helping me to integrate my German/British Jewish/Christian roots. They have given me an understanding of the suffering of non-Jewish people affected by the Hitler regime and the courage of those who resisted Hitler's pogroms. Our friendships freed me from negative feelings of past events. This has enabled me to write freely.

I can now echo words attributed to C. G. Jung: '*I am not what happened to me. I am what I choose to become.*'

Finally I want to thank Helen Porter, Hannah Torjussen, and the rest of the team at DLT for their work in enabling us to launch *The Deeper Centre*.

FOREWORD

THIS INSPIRING book, which will enrich and enthral you, is the story of a rebellious Jewish girl who became a committed Roman Catholic nun, working on the edges of society to offer love and compassion where there has often been only fear and pain. Sister Eva Heymann SHCJ has also accompanied many on their journeys of faith, sometimes on the threshold of life and death. The following pages are filled with moving and poetic recollections of Sister Eva's ministry on the margins, taking us deeper into the centre of divine love and helping to reconnect us more meaningfully with our own ventures of faith. In her late seventies, Eva refuses to take the line of least resistance and still makes herself available for others, in person, by telephone or through e-mail. She thinks nothing of flying to America to lead a retreat beside the Californian pines or of spending six days in solitary retreat in the wilds of Wales before driving back to London, through the Forest of Dean, to rehearse for a performance of Haydn's *Creation*.

I first met Eva when I went to interview her for the *Sunday* programme on BBC Radio 4. We chatted in a tiny attic room of her London convent, adorned with cyclamen, postcards of trees and the fragrance of beeswax. There, over peppermint tea and chocolate biscuits, I learned how Eva, the youngest of three, had been born into a nominally Jewish family in Germany in 1927. Her father had been an engineer who specialised in building electric power stations. In 1933, with the Hitler movement gathering momentum, Eva's father was removed from his job and had to retire early. When she was nine, Eva moved with her family to Freiburg in the Black Forest where she developed a natural affinity with the whole of creation, especially trees. But darkness was on the horizon. After the *Kristallnacht* of 1938, when scores of German synagogues were burnt to the ground along with numerous Jewish homes and shops, the Heymanns found themselves caught up in the pogroms. Signs declaring 'Jews Forbidden' prevented families like theirs from going into food shops. Eva was not allowed to attend school and could not use the new local swimming baths at the bottom of her road. 'Life was restricted and fearful,' she told me. 'I grew up with the horror of the concentration camps and the fear that any one of our family might end up there. We began to realise that people were disappearing, not to be heard of again.'

In the spring of 1939, Eva and her sister, Lotte, found asylum in England. They were placed with different Christian families in Oxford. A few months later their parents left Germany and were eventually reunited with their daughters three weeks before the outbreak of the second world war. Eva's brother, Dick, who had been sent to the safety of Switzerland, joined them later. As a refugee in Britain at the age of eleven, Eva experienced new forms of alienation as she adapted to English culture. As a recalcitrant teenager and a depressed adolescent, she reached a point where she did not want to go on living. She admits she touched 'rock bottom' but managed to surface again, finding meaning to her life through a nascent journey in faith. After spending the first 20 years of her life without any spiritual practice or sense of belief in the transcendent, she began to pray spontaneously: 'If there is a God, show me.' There were no immediate results. But the stirrings of an answer emerged while she was studying for a diploma in social science. 'Reading philosophy, I began to have a sense that there was a being greater than the evil I had experienced,' she went on. 'That resonated with my need to love and be loved, and to know something about the source of love.'

One of Eva's closest friends happened to be a Roman Catholic. While the pair had their disagreements about faith and religion, the friend helped sow in Eva the idea that God loved humankind so much that he had chosen to enter its world and become one with it. The mystery of such love was beyond Eva's rational understanding but gradually became a reality in the realm of faith. At the same time her own suffering and her own family losses – relatives who had died in the Nazi terror camps – led her to conclude that suffering and new birth formed part of an inextricable paradox. The secret lay in the incarnation, in the very embodiment of God, and Eva longed to know more about the divine artist who had 'entered into our mess' and embraced what she saw as the chaos within her. What drew her to the Roman Catholic Church was the fact that it was an institution which had 'survived through centuries, despite many public scandals and sinfulness'. She felt there would be 'room for me and my own chaotic history'.

Eventually Eva was received into the Roman Catholic Church. Then, in 1957, at the age of thirty, with a diploma and teaching experience behind her, she joined the Society of the Holy Child Jesus, a religious congregation that had been founded by an American woman, Cornelia Connelly, in 1846. Life on those uncharted waters was rarely plain sailing but Eva felt she had a strong calling to commit herself to Christ in that congregation. She worked mainly as a teacher – she was head of a girls' boarding school in Sussex – and as a psychiatric social worker, before spending ten years as a volunteer with the Terrence Higgins Trust, the first HIV/AIDS agency in Britain. She later became a volunteer at the day centre of the Mildmay Mission Hospital which supports people living with HIV/AIDS. She also assisted women and children seeking asylum in Britain, identifying with their feelings of displacement, and she has been long involved in spiritual direction and retreat work.

'I think all my life I have lived on the edge, partly through circumstances and to a greater degree by choice,' she explained. 'Although I have worked in the ecumenical world for some time, my own feeling is that it is through interfaith dialogue that we begin to see the inclusiveness of God's love. When I think of the contribution the eastern mystics give our age, and the connectedness between science and religion, the institution might appear, dare I say, almost irrelevant. But we do need institutions that have a degree of flexibility and vision, institutions that can allow something of Christ's mercy and compassion to shine through, institutions that are prepared to take risks as God did in becoming one of us.'

The Deeper Centre is a book which arises out of the risks Eva herself has taken in her journey of faith. Set against a tree-lined panorama, these reflections trace the contours of her own rugged pilgrimage, offering perceptive insights into the worlds of doubt and faith, alienation and belonging, brokenness and healing. And to the very core of these meditations the redemptive love of God penetrates.

It has often struck Eva that there is a general hunger in the world for faith in God, but there are also understandable reasons why many people do not feel at home within existing institutional organisations. Faith was absent from her life for the first 20 years and there have since been many periods when it has been fragile. There are still moments when Eva, like many of us, cries out: 'Where are you, God?' But she is aware that God is not phased by such uncertainties. God's time scale is different from ours. She has discovered that God believes in her even when her own belief in God wavers.

The disruption of leaving the family home in Germany all those years ago has echoes for Eva of the desert experiences of her Jewish ancestors. Uprooted from the familiar rhythms of daily life, they became aware of their faith growing through a gradual intellectual assimilation of the wasteland experience. Yet it was not merely the outward surroundings, but the *inner awareness* of God's presence that sharpened their spiritual focus. This has also been Eva's experience not only as a refugee and a foreigner in a strange environment but also as an outsider in many different situations. Through these experiences she has learnt to reach out to those on the margins of society and the church. There are many who seek faith, she observes, but cannot commit themselves to traditional church communities. Some have been ostracised because of their colour or sexual orientation. Others feel frustrated that the signs of hope generated by the second Vatican council have not been developed as fully as they had expected.

'When I was asked to write a book, my immediate response was to laugh derisively as Sarai did when a heavenly messenger foretold that she would give birth to a son despite her old age,' Eva tells me. 'I could identify with Sarai's reaction. The invitation to write seemed to come too late in my life. I was being asked to make a leap into the unknown – and I was fearful. But faced with such a challenge, I did not recoil from bargaining with God in the tradition of my forefathers. I, too, needed to have some reassurance as a sign that this new venture would have his blessing.'

Eva has always loved trees and, as she walked through the countryside trying to overcome an early outbreak of writer's block, she suddenly remembered an essay by the German poet Hermann Hesse. He had once written about a tree which actually spoke, exclaiming that 'a kernel is hidden in me, a spark, a thought from eternal life. The attempt and the risk the eternal mother took with me is unique. I was made to reveal the eternal in my smallest detail.' Those sentences silenced Eva. Trees had always comforted her, stilled her hasty thoughts, listened to her complaints as well as helped to share her excitements and joys. They had challenged her to acknowledge that God's love is at work in all of us throughout our lives. But that day, on her walk through the woods, Eva realised that Hesse had gone further by pointing out that *God needs us to reveal him to others*. It was a breakthrough, a *kairos* moment.

FOREWORD

As Eva sat down at her computer and began to summon up the words, she soon found herself being put in touch with hidden feelings and lost memories. At times the process of writing was painful but at the same time cathartic because it 'released my inner child to play, recall and relive long-forgotten episodes of my life'. There was, for her, also the sense that 'doors that have been locked can now be opened.' She received this as 'the sheer gift of ageing, having at last the freedom to dare to be oneself, owning the dark as well as the light that penetrates the mystery of our being'.

Published as Eva looks forward to her eightieth birthday and the fiftieth anniversary of her entering the Society of the Holy Child Jesus, this book is a unique spiritual tapestry woven from the multicoloured fibres of an extraordinary life. It is the touching memoir of one person's search for God – and for her deepest identity. Through the authentic telling of her own faith story, Eva Heymann encourages us to look again at our own. Like a good spiritual director, she knows that the secrets always lie within.

MICHAEL FORD
The Quantocks
February 2006

1

CHRISTMAS TREES

*A tree says: a kernel is hidden within
me, a spark, a thought from eternal life.*[1]

Hermann Hesse

THROUGHOUT MY LIFE, trees have been significant. They were my friends in times of need, my teachers, my healers. They were the first created beings in whom I could place my trust: trees heard me – not with ears like people, but as silent beings who were never too busy to listen. I felt at home with them – and shared my joys and sorrows with them. There was a real sense of being in relationship not only with trees, but with the whole of nature in all its manifold wonder.

Reliving some of our early memories can help us to use these as a foundation for our ongoing search for meaning in life. This continues to be my own experience and I hope that in sharing it with others, it may also encourage them to undertake a similar exploration.

My first encounter with the mystery of trees stems from our family's celebration of Christmas in Germany. We were nominally Jewish, living in Breslau. The city was renamed Wroclawia when parts of Eastern Germany were ceded to Poland after the second world war. My father came from an orthodox Jewish background and my mother from a more liberal Jewish family. Neither was a practising Jew when my brother, sister and I were born. My father decided we could choose our own religious paths if we so desired. Looking back this liberalism seems extraordinary, because in every other respect he was stern, authoritarian and feared – especially by my brother and me.

I have never fully understood how it came to be that we celebrated Christmas each year, with the most beautifully decorated tree. I was dimly aware that Christmas was linked to a special birthday celebration but it was a long while before I discovered whose birthday it was. In my perplexity I wrote to the Christ child asking for gifts!

At one level there might well be a simple reason for our Christmas celebration: it was important for my father that we shared the same social and ethical customs which formed part of the lives of many of his professional colleagues and closest friends. In that sense, Christmas was an external feast like many other events. Yet, for me, it became an inner journey of discovery which, even to this day, continues to lead me to a deeper understanding of Christ's birth and entry into our world. I can identify with Hesse's words: 'A tree says: a kernel is hidden within me, a spark, a thought from eternal life.' There is a suggestion of mystery in that thought, which I find challenging. We often think of mystery in terms of darkness, and that can be scary. But if we dare to explore the darkness, we might find a light that is brighter than daylight. Life itself is a risky journey which presents us with the juxtaposition of darkness and light, the rough and the smooth, laughter and tears.

Each day offers new opportunities to explore the wonder of our being. Our energies are often directed into the activities of our outer world, but we need time and space to explore the deeper realities of our inner world. A tree cannot live unless it is connected with its roots – and neither can you and I. We too need to be connected with the roots of our being. As we attempt to make that journey we may grow in experience and understanding of our own and other people's faith journeys with all their ups and downs, light and shade, sorrows and joys.

Some years ago I came across an ancient Chinese proverb which has helped to make sense of the labyrinthine ways of my ongoing journey in faith: 'The present moment is the outcome of the past and the foundation of the future.'[2] Whenever I find myself in darkness, in the face of ongoing difficulties in my life, I explore past experiences and often discover that this sheds light on my confusion and inner storms. I think that this can be helpful whether we have faith or not. But, as a person with faith, I believe that the Holy Spirit dwelling within us can guide us through many dark periods. The outcome may not be what we initially hoped for – we often want instant revelation – but ultimately the insights we receive help us to integrate the past and the future. This may not change the actual events but it gives us a different view and interpretation.

Let me tell you a little more about our family Christmas celebrations.

During the morning of 24 December every year, a Christmas tree was placed in our sitting room. The tip of the highest branch seemed to touch the ceiling. I still wonder how such a tall tree could have been manoeuvred through doors and stairs without damage to itself or to our furniture. I think it took several men to achieve this feat. We three children were banned from the room all day while my mother and our cook, Elise, together with other helpers, decorated the branches.

In Germany Christmas celebrations start on Christmas Eve. We waited impatiently for that moment, after six o'clock, when the double doors of our sitting room would be opened and we would see the tree in all its glory with brightly coloured wax candles lit and flickering. All other lights were turned off. It was a glittering spectacle and never failed to fill me with wonder and delight. On such occasions the most fitting verbal response was a deep 'aaahhh', followed by a moment of silence. The fact that I was so small and the tree was so tall was not daunting because all of us were transformed by the dancing lights and the joyfulness of the occasion. Sometimes people refer to such moments as 'magical'. But that was not what I experienced and I think I would be right in assuming that other members of my family would not have thought of it as magical either. Real beauty tends to silence us, if only for a moment.

We were dressed in our best party clothes and it seemed perfectly appropriate that the tree was also adorned and transformed. The candlelight was reflected in the long silver strands which draped the branches. It seemed to me that the tree welcomed and beckoned us to come closer. There were the sweet temptations of marzipan fruits, as well as the allure of all kinds of other sweets and special Christmas biscuits in the shape of stars hanging from every limb of the tree. Every year it was a unique moment – unlike any other experience. We sang traditional German Christmas carols before receiving and opening our presents. It was a real family occasion and the only one of its kind which I treasure, remembering it as a time when everyone seemed relaxed and happy.

More than half a century later, what does this scene evoke in me now? Surprisingly, a sense of wonder and curiosity. I want to stay for a while with the tree and its flickering, dancing lights. As a young child, I could allow myself to be enfolded in the mystery and that was sufficient for the time being. To be present was a gift in itself. There are moments when the gap between past and present can appear to merge. I sometimes feel that the seven-year-old me has yet much to teach me about those meaningful experiences from my younger years. Children often have an ability to enter into mystical experiences, but they may not have the vocabulary to express it. That could, I suppose, diminish the experience, but I am inclined to think it may actually enhance it. I know that for me it was a reality unlike any other. That in itself was sufficient and it was reassuring that the experience would be repeated year after year. In those days there were no menacing shadows on the horizon.

Later in life, I had similar feelings of amazement when I watched spectacular sunrises and sunsets. These too are encounters of phenomenal light and beauty that can touch us in the depth of our being but cannot easily be described verbally. When we stop to reflect on them, we can glean something of the meaning of Hermann Hesse's words. The tree seemed to have the power to convey its message. But the richness of the symbolism became clear to me only many years later, when I was beginning to explore the possibility of the existence of God. I find myself smiling as I write this, because it highlights how often our human sense of time is so very different to God's timing. We hurry through each day, seldom stopping to reflect on what we have seen or heard and what has touched us: 'What is this life if, full of care, we have no time to stand and stare?'[3] But God makes time, as gardeners do. He works within us, carefully preparing the ground of our inner being before selecting the seeds he wants to sow. Every gardener knows the soil has to be tilled, nourished and freed from weeds and other obstacles which could damage the tiny seeds. Once placed into the darkness of the soil, the seeds may have to wait a long time before they see the light of day and are transformed into their respective flowers or fruits or trees. A similar process takes place in our faith journeys. There may be long periods of darkness, while the seeds of faith seem to be hibernating, waiting for the call to break open and taking the risk to grow and reach their potential. In retrospect, I believe that the annual Christmas celebrations during my early years prepared the ground for my ongoing journey in faith.

As I relive the hours spent around our Christmas tree, I am struck again by the importance of colour in my life. The candles evoke many feelings about the symbolism of colour. Several years ago, I was in contact with blind and partially sighted children. They taught me how to 'see' many things in a new way. I asked them once what colour meant for them and they soon enlightened me. Red was tasty, like strawberries and cherries. Green was like the feel of grass, especially in the early spring when the blades are tender. Blue was like the water in the swimming pool – cool but not cold. Brown was earthy and, though not as bright as some other colours, it had a special quality because it was the ground where the seeds of new life wait to grow. Yellow was like lemon, sometimes sharp but also bright like sunshine. It was a new experience for me to relate to colours in that way, but it enhanced my own appreciation of their natural spectrum. Now as I think back to the candles on our Christmas tree, I am able to interpret their colours in many different ways. The children whose sight was impaired opened my eyes to a new understanding. Their vision was deeper and more comprehensive than mine. They made me aware of our connectedness with our surroundings and, above all, with one another.

We are contingent beings, and it is in sharing our thoughts, hopes and fears that we can become channels of light for each other. Life would be dull if it were not possible to discover continually the meaning of God's message: 'Now I am making the whole of creation new.'[4] As we age, we can become weary or even sceptical of such sayings, but children are sometimes wiser than we are. They can trust and hope that good things will happen. Sadly, this trust can be eroded by later life experiences. But during those early years of my life I learnt that I could experience a quality of joy and a sense of security that felt reassuring. When those sitting room doors were opened on Christmas Eve, we could once again enter into the light. That mattered to me for, like many children, I was often afraid of the dark. The fact that there were no other lights in the room, except for the candles on the tree, enabled all of us to focus on the wonder and beauty of candlelight. Each little candle was only about three inches high but a supply of unlit candles was always there to replace the ones that were burning down. This was a ritual. Every new candle was lit from the diminishing stump to give a sense of continuity.

At the time I would not have been able to link the symbolism of light with the image of Christ, the Light of the World. That awareness came many years later. However, the yearly impact of our Christmas tree made me realise that even one candle can dispel darkness, but the multiplicity of candlelight seemed to transform not only the room but each one of us, so that for a while there was real harmony between us – unlike any other time. The very fact that I can still summon up those feelings of Christmas peace and joy encourages me to think that the tiniest flickers of light can be kindled into flames of love and hope. The Christmas tree is not only a memory of the past, but is potentially a bearer of good news now and for the future.

There is a mysterious process in our faith journeys. When I first heard that Christmas was connected with the birth of Christ, I asked who Christ was and why he was so important that his birthday was celebrated all over the world. The answers I got did not satisfy me but I sensed that, one day, I would eventually be led to discover this for myself. The intriguing character of 'questions and answers' is that, in the realm of spirituality, each answer appears to lead us to yet another question. This process seems to bring us deeper and closer to the ultimate truth which will be revealed when we pass through death into eternal life. There are times when it seems an interminable journey, like finding the right path in a tangled wood, with intertwined tracks and no clear signposts. At such moments it might be helpful to stop and rest a while, remembering, as I mentioned earlier, past experiences which have been life giving and can still be sources of reassurance in moments of confusion.

Looking back on the early years of my life, I am grateful for the many good experiences I can still recall and relive. I am sure this is generally true for all of us, though our memories will be coloured by our individual uniqueness. No two people will see, hear or feel things in the same way. This is likewise true in nature. For instance, when one walks through a wood or an orchard, even though the trees may be of one single species, there will not be any two trees that are identical. Each one lives out of its own root system and those roots are usually out of sight, deep within the earth which nourishes them. They may be touched by underground streams of water and fed by the experiences which become rooted in us – invisible roots which supply us with strength to grow and become the unique being we are destined to be. In times of danger and trouble, we can draw strength from our roots, just as trees do.

It was only many years after we had left Breslau that I mused on another aspect of our annual Christmas trees. I was revisiting Freiburg, where we had lived for a short time. The city is on the edge of the Black Forest, so named because it is a vast area of pine trees which gives it a dark and mysterious atmosphere. When we were there, I used to wonder if some of the trees were perhaps distant cousins of our Christmas trees in Breslau. They were like huge evergreen giants. Unlike other trees, they did not have leaves or fruits which could be eaten by people or by birds and other woodland creatures. They were stern and unbending, but I grew to love and respect them as friends and wise companions. When the summer sun penetrated the inner darkness of the woodland, the rays made beautiful patterns on the ground and sometimes lit up the tree trunks in a startling way, transforming them into sentinels of light.

Recently, while walking again through the forest, I rested for a while on a fallen tree trunk. I was not the only one there. Insects were scurrying through the moss and birds were chirping. As I looked upwards, I could see to the top of the branches, patterned like a crown under the blue sky above. For a moment I had a sense of the reality of eternity, even though it seemed far beyond my reach. I was spellbound by the beauty and the power of the tree as well as the penetrating light above me. I wondered: 'How did you grow so tall and straight?' It was a long time before the reply registered in my thoughts: 'I was drawn by the light to fulfil my destiny.' I find these words inspiring and still vividly remember the impact of the light that day. I sat there for a long and silent time and let my thoughts take me back to the flickering, dancing lights of the candles on our Christmas tree.

Such reflective thinking can give strength and meaning to our present moments especially when we need light to dispel our inner darkness. They also remind me of the Chinese proverb about the present moment being linked with our past and how our awareness of that will enable us to gain courage to move towards the future.

Thousands of candles can be lit
from a single candle,
and the life of the candle will not be shortened.
Happiness never decreases by being shared.[5]

2

STARS

Let God speak within you and your thoughts will grow silent.[1]

Hermann Hesse

SEE STARS as distant lights in the outer darkness. At various times I have also experienced them as flickers of light in my own inner darkness. As a child, I enjoyed eating the edible stars from our Christmas tree. Now I have many different visions of stars. For instance, in our celebrity culture people who achieve outstanding results in sport or are enshrined through television fame, are stars. So are artists, musicians and indeed anyone especially gifted. These images can become very confusing. But Hermann Hesse invites me to be still. Metaphorically the shutters of our windows which open towards the outer world can momentarily be closed. When we re-open them, we may find that ostensibly nothing has changed, but our inner perception of the outer world may well have altered.

Stillness is hard to achieve in our busy and often

noisy world. Living in London makes me aware of that. Even during the night I can be wakened by the sound of police cars with their sirens screaming. But it is not only exterior sounds which bombard us. Unresolved worries and anxieties can manifest their own discords within us throughout day and night. The inner voice of fear is one which I have often found most difficult to defuse. Sometimes it may seem appropriate to confront it, but I prefer to find that space within me where I can listen to other sounds and see different sights. And I do not regard this as a form of escapism.

Recently, when I allowed myself some time for quiet reflection, I began to think about people who have helped me in my past and present life journeys. I was standing near the open window of my room and I looked up at the starlit sky. Stars have always fascinated me. I began to become aware that I could also call to mind a symbolic mixture of stars, in the form of people. Some of them were distant and others relatively close; several were in clusters but others were alone. Although I only knew some of these by name, all of them have been stars at various times in my life. Most of them would be surprised to learn the effect they had on me.

The first star is an unknown woman, a wealthy Austrian friend of Hitler's. An unlikely star, but without her, many Jewish children would not have been able to leave Germany and the occupied countries. Hitler asked her for a considerable gift of money. Initially the woman refused his request, but later bargained with him. She promised him a substantial sum, provided he would allow Jewish children from Germany, Czechoslovakia and Austria to emigrate. Hitler was reluctant to accept her terms, but he needed money urgently, so he conceded. As a result, the 'Kinder Transports' (Children's Transports) were speedily organised over a period of several months. Every fortnight, Jewish children left Germany for different places in England. My sister and I were among these, and were offered foster homes in Oxford.

The plans of the unknown woman also brought into being a cluster of stars. These were the Jewish refugee committees in England and Germany. The committees worked under pressure of time to find suitable homes and to ensure that the designated foster parents would be able to finance the refugees. These families appear to me as clusters of stars shining in a dark sky. Finding safe havens for the children, some as young as two years old, required considerable organisation. Many of the children were traumatised by the events in Germany and all of them faced the possibility that they might never see their own families again. Looking back to those dark times, I am aware that the counter sign to Hitler's atrocities was the compassion this generated in large numbers of people. Such human responses continue to be light in our world which has so many areas of terrible darkness.

As I recall these events, I am very aware that even one person can affect the lives of hundreds of people. Hitler succeeded in bringing about the most horrendous suffering to millions of human beings. One woman's actions to counteract this assured a safe passage into life to a substantial number of young people, who in turn could become life-givers to future generations.

The second star is a teacher at the school my sister and I attended in Germany. She took a risk, which could have had serious consequences for her. I will never forget her courage. Early one afternoon, she called us out of class and told us to go straight home but, like the kings who followed the star in the Christmas story, we had to go by a different route. We set off, puzzled and bewildered. It was only when we arrived home that we heard of the terrible atrocities which had happened. It was the day of *Kristallnacht*, so called because Hitler decreed that throughout Germany the windows of Jewish shops and homes should be shattered. The fury against Jews had been simmering for a long time, but the murder of a German diplomat by a Jewish teenager in Paris gave Hitler the opportunity he had been waiting for. From that moment on, he began to ignite a roaring fire of hatred. Had Lotte and I taken our usual route from school to our home, we would have been caught up in the violence and systematic arrests as well as the burning of the synagogue. Pogroms against Jews began in earnest.

I have never forgotten this teacher who risked so much to help us at a time of unprecedented crisis. I visualise her amongst a cluster of stars, too many to count, for I have realised that her courage was echoed by many other German people. We should never talk in a collective sense when we recall the atrocities of the persecution. In Germany, and later in neighbouring countries which were invaded by Hitler, small but powerful resistance movements were formed. They too shone like bright stars in a dark sky. Although some of their stories have been told, the majority of these brave people are unsung heroes. They have made me aware not to make a generalised judgement on any group or nation. I will never condone Hitler's murder of six million Jews, nor the large number of homosexual people as well as gypsies and handicapped men, women and children, who died in camps. But neither will I use the generic term 'the Germans', knowing, as I do now, how many individual people had the courage of their convictions to resist the horrors that were perpetrated in their name. But it has been a long inner journey for me to reach this point. I realise now, that for all of us who have had hurtful and life-threatening experiences, the process of healing and forgiveness can take a lifetime.

As I recall these experiences again, I am aware that they shed light on a deep-seated inclination to relive the past. This is probably common to all who have been traumatised by events in their lives. We need to share our experiences with someone who can listen and help us to make sense of painful situations. But at the same time we also need to move on and reach a point in our own journey when we can harness our past hurts in a more constructive way. I feel privileged knowing that the integration of past experiences has enabled me to move forward with a vision of hope. Throughout my adult life I have worked with disadvantaged men, women and children from all parts of the world. They have taught me more about living and loving than any books I have read. They, too, are part of the starlight which shines through the bitterness of our lives.

But the stars in my life have not always been connected with crisis. I have known many people who would never think of themselves as stars. Most of them would simply see themselves as ordinary folk. But the ordinary has the potential to be extraordinary. Two such stars are a married couple who offered me living space in their house when I started my first teaching post at a primary school in 1948. I had a bed-sitting room, my own kitchenette and the use of their bathroom. For this Mr and Mrs Davies charged me the equivalent of £1.50 per week! Even by the standards of that time, this was extraordinarily cheap. They were a unique couple in many ways, not least because they were active members of the Communist Party whose weekly meetings were held at their house. I was intrigued by the way they greeted each one as they arrived: 'Welcome brother' or 'Hello sister'. They never spoke with me about their political views, but Mrs Davies would occasionally show me recipes in the *Daily Worker*. In return I would point out interesting nature articles from my newspaper. Neither of us ever mentioned that we found other interesting articles in each other's papers. I wondered if Mrs Davies hoped I might develop an interest in communism, but she never referred openly to their political ideals. I trusted their integrity.

Mrs Davies was an ideal landlady. I felt sure that, after a while, my rent would be raised because other people in similar 'digs' were paying considerably more than I did. So when she came to me one day and said, 'Bill and I have been thinking about the rent,' I was not surprised. She continued: 'You're away most weekends, so it doesn't seem right to charge you £1.50. We'll put it down to £1.00 per week.' Some of my sceptical friends said that this might be a ruse to get me into the Communist Party, but that was not the case.

At that stage of my journey through life I was beginning to become interested in Christianity. I felt that this couple lived their political beliefs in a similar way to members of early Christian communities. Mr and Mrs

Davies shared what they had not only with their Communist Party siblings, but also with neighbours and friends and anyone in need, regardless of race, colour or religious belief. I was impressed by their integrity and sense of justice. For them, communism was a commitment to work for those who lived below acceptable standards and who had little hope that their circumstances would ever change. Moreover, they had personal experience of the years of depression in Wales. Both their families had been dealt severe blows by poverty and unemployment. I saw in their lives something which I recognised as an aspect of Christ's own life: a love for the poor and rejected as well as a desire to challenge the political and religious institutions of his time. Mr and Mrs Davies remain as bright stars continuing to challenge me to live a life of integrity. I still remember them as people who had the courage of their convictions and acted on this in their service of others. At that time, as a woman in my twenties, I admired these qualities. Even half a century later, their light beckons at times when I am confronted by many of the current problems of the consumer society in which we live. As far as I know, the couple had no religious affiliations, but they will continue to be lights for me and an inspiration to 'act justly, to love tenderly and to walk humbly with your God'.[2]

The fourth star in this constellation is Horge. He was eleven when I met him a few years ago. He and his mother were referred to me for counselling. Horge's father had died recently from an AIDS-related illness. His mother also had AIDS-related health problems. Horge was their only child. Intelligent and sensitive, he initially spent most of the sessions drawing pictures of

Star Wars. It was not difficult to interpret these images as a means of depicting how his own life had become a struggle for survival against unknown odds. On one occasion, Horge brought his guitar to our session. He explained that his mother was feeling unwell. He often played for her to soothe her pain. As she lay curled up in a chair, he started to serenade. It was a moving experience to see how she soon relaxed and drifted off to sleep. Afterwards I asked him what he had played. He said it was an 'étude' but he was not sure what that word meant. I told him it was a French word meaning 'study'. As soon as his mother woke, he asked her if she knew the meaning of 'étude' and was proud to be able to explain it to her. This was perhaps just a small indication of how Horge was taking on the role of carer for his mother. Understandably, both of them found it difficult to talk about future plans for Horge. We agreed that we would have some sessions for each of them on their own. Horge told me that he wanted to assure his mother that, in spite of his grief, he knew he had a future. When we met together again, he spoke about a family picnic he had enjoyed when his father was still alive. He explained that he had been very young then – about five years old. Turning to his mother he said: 'When I was little, we all went out together in the car. Dad drove, you were the navigator and I was the baby in the back seat. Now you drive and I'm the navigator and there is no baby in the back seat. But one day I'll drive and my girlfriend will be the navigator and we'll have a baby in the back seat!' Both of them cried and my own tears flowed too. But the message had been received and it was now possible for the mother and Horge to look forward to his future with hope. Shortly after this, his mother became seriously ill and had to go into hospital, so her sister, who lived in Switzerland, came to stay with Horge. Horge had decided he would like to live with her and her family after his mother's death. Once again, he took responsibility for the most difficult choice. His question was about whether he should stay with his mother until she died or whether it would be better for both of them if they said their good-byes while she was still conscious. They agreed this would be best.

I have worked with children most of my life, but Horge stands out as a shining star in a most grim situa-tion. I have learnt that children have a wisdom of their own which is often beyond our understanding. Horge reminded me of a sapling, already rooted but struggling to grow towards the light. When one encounters this inner life force there is a real sense that we are on holy ground. I believe that the strength given to Horge and his mother came from a deeper source than our own human resources. When Horge said goodbye to me, he said: 'I have to start a new life now, but my mum and dad will always be part of that.' Horge's mother died peacefully soon afterwards.

Sacrificial love is surely the deepest and purest form of love. Working with Horge and his mother made me very aware of that. Such love is eternal. Horge's parents were 'drug users' and that would have been the label attached to them by many people. But such a stigma conveys more about the people who confer labels than the ones whom they denigrate. Yes, Horge's parents were drug users, but there was also a great deal of love in that family. I am inclined to think that, from the time he was born, Horge generated love for his parents. That may well have been his mission in life. This family shines like a trio of small stars. They bring to life Isaiah's prophecy of the incarnation: ' ... calf and lion cub feed together with a little boy to lead them.'[3] This quotation brings me back to the Christmas tree and the birth of Christ.

The mythology of stars has always played a meaningful part in this. The journeys of the wise men who left their homes and followed a star is well known. We are equally familiar with the story of the angels who appeared to the shepherds on the hills near Bethlehem. I want to stay with both these stories and explore their relevance for us today.

We are looking at two groups of people who are very different from each other. The wise men or kings were probably astrologers. They were able to find their way to Bethlehem by their knowledge of the stars. Throughout the ages, stars have provided travellers on land and sea with direction for their excursions. The kings felt called to make their journey and present the baby with precious and meaningful gifts. We can only imagine the meeting of these two groups: on the one hand there were the wise men and on the other the baby with Mary and Joseph. This paradoxical encounter touches my heart whenever I recall that first Christmas. The moment when the kings took off their crowns and worshipped the baby who was to become king of the universe is for me one of the most challenging visualisations of the nativity. It is a moment when the earthly dignitaries demonstrated their wisdom of knowing that their material riches paled before the love which emanated from the tiny baby held in Mary's arms. Christ's entry into our world overturned many of our value systems. I like to think that when the kings left their gifts behind and travelled back to their own homes, they were richer than they had ever been because they had been touched by Love incarnate. Once they left the cave of the nativity, they were enveloped again in the darkness of the outer world. But inwardly they were renewed by Light eternal. This too can be our experience when we meditate on the wonder of Christ's birth and his desire to find space in our hearts.

The second group of visitors to see the new-born baby were in sharp contrast to the kings. They were shepherds, traditionally at the bottom of the social order of their times. Their work isolated them from the rest of the community, as they had to guard their flocks day and night. Yet both groups had something in common: they received a heavenly message about the birth of Christ. What does this say to us? I think it is a very simple but profound revelation, namely that God speaks to us where we are and as we are. He speaks to the kings through their knowledge and study of the stars. But he reveals himself to the shepherds on their own ground: the hillside familiar to them. The heavenly music which they heard and the vision of angels which they saw filled them with spontaneous joy. Their response was immediate: 'Let us go and worship him!'

This has echoes for me in my own journey of faith. I first discovered the presence of God through my love and connectedness with the wonders of nature: in trees, fields and flowers. God came to me in my wild days, when I struggled hard to avoid any form of institutional religion. He found me where I was and waited for me to recognise him as the Love I longed for.

STARS

We are made holy
By our recognition of God in us.
God is in all and everything.
But the reality of God's presence
Only comes about
Through human recognition.
Ah then, we have the power
To sacralize the world.[4]

3

BIRTH

I was made to form and reveal the eternal in my smallest special detail.[1]

Hermann Hesse

IF TREES COULD SPEAK, I think these words might have been spoken by one of the Christmas trees from my early childhood. Birth is shrouded in mystery. That is true in the realm of nature as well as in the evolution of human beings. Our uniqueness is hidden deep within us and it takes a lifetime to discover the potential richness of the seed from which we have grown. With this in mind, I would like to reflect on the significance of Christ's birth. Like the shepherds who were given this news, I too want to go to Bethlehem and 'see this thing that has happened which the Lord has made known to us.'[2]

In the first chapter I recalled some memories of joy and peace in our celebration of Christmas in Breslau. But there is more to this story than merely a happy childhood memory. Celebrating Christ's birthday has an ongoing significance for us now. It is a reminder that God offers us the possibility of peace and love, not only as a promise for the future, but as a reality in our present life. The symbolism of the Christmas tree deepens my awareness of the meaning of Christ's birth. I recall the majesty of the tall tree which had been uprooted and cut from its familiar surroundings and then stood glorified in our sitting room. It spoke without words but conveyed the power of love which it represented. For me it is also an ongoing image of Christ's willingness to be uprooted and to enter into our finite world.

There is another symbol hidden in Hesse's words. They reflect Mary's experience. A seed was indeed planted in her at the annunciation. She could truly identify with Hesse's thoughts: 'I was made to form and reveal the eternal in my smallest special detail.'

For centuries, writers, musicians and artists have tried to express the mystery of the incarnation. The only way I can begin to grasp that event is to sit in silent expectation. Often words can obstruct the way when I am confronted with something I find difficult to understand. When that happens, I turn to music or art to enable me to go deeper than words and help me to enter into the hidden truths of God's relationship with us. Each year I choose a favourite picture which I use for meditation during Advent. This year it is La Tour's *The New-born*. This picture leads me from the relentless buzzing of thoughts in my head to a deeper place where there is stillness. There I can reflect on what the picture conveys to me at this time in my life. I have discovered that every present moment has a hidden gift, provided I am open to receive it. The picture depicts three persons: Mary is cradling Jesus on her lap, supporting him with her arms; another woman has a candle in her left hand and is using the right one to shield the baby from the flame. Behind them is darkness. It could be the stable or cave where Jesus was born. The painting communicates harmony in the soft terracotta coloured gowns worn by Mary and the unknown woman. This blends with the serenity of the candlelight. It enables me to quieten my restless thoughts.

The first thing that strikes me is that there are neither sounds nor harsh lights – only the flicker of the candle held by the older woman whose eyes, like Mary's, are totally fixed on the baby. I feel I can watch the scene from the shadows beyond the light. There I can be close to the three central figures, without being intrusive. I am silenced by Mary's expression. She is calm, yet it seems to me that she is almost bewildered by the awesome truth that the incarnate son of God is lying in her own arms. Words from Psalm 19:3 come to mind: 'No utterance at all, no speech, no sound' can be heard as we contemplate with Mary the miracle of Christ's birth. I am touched by a human factor in Mary. She still appears to be a little inexperienced in holding her baby. Her hands and fingers have not yet relaxed and I feel that the older woman, who may have assisted her with the birth, is there to give Mary ongoing support. Her presence, and the gesture of her hand shielding the baby from direct candlelight, convey a protectiveness towards mother and child. I resonate with Mary's vulnerability. Humanly speaking, nothing could have prepared her for the reality of this moment in time. The seed sown in Mary's womb has burst into life. To be able to recognise this is Love's unsolicited gift to each of us.

In the light of that candle and that event, we need space for silent adoration.

La Tour's painting evokes a real sense of peace in me. For a while at least, I can be totally myself, without pretence or fear. In the presence of this child and his mother, I can allow myself to be led to a deeper level of faith than usual. Every new-born baby is a little miracle, but here and now I can acknowledge Christ as God and man, divine and human. That is a miracle like no other. So often my faith wavers. But here, in this stillness, there is nothing to divert or distract me. Like Mary and the other woman, I feel drawn into silent adoration. Such moments are vital, because they remain rooted in me. I can revive them to renew my relation-ship with Christ when I have allowed myself to become distanced from him through the rush and pressures of daily life.

The candle sheds its light mostly on Mary. She is gazing at her son with profound tenderness. Although his eyes are closed, there seems to be a deep communi-cation between them. The rest of the room is in darkness. There is no light where I am, but the light of the candle invites me to draw closer. I have always loved candles. I explained in the first chapter how the ones on our Christmas tree spoke to me in many ways. Later I saw them as symbols of light in a dark world. Now before this picture, I am aware that even a tiny flame can transform a dark stable into a heavenly place. I am moved by the light which shines on the baby. He is utterly at peace and it is hard not to imagine that I can see and hear him breathing! The juxtaposition of the Light of the World in Mary's arms and the brightness of lights, which each Christmas season blaze in the decorations of our main streets, makes me reflect more deeply. I am beginning to realise that Christ seeks to be born in small hearts, often where we least expect to find him. He does not need the proliferation of electrical displays, but he still seeks to find a place where one candle can make all the difference.

More than other pictures I know, this one conveys to me the frailty of the baby and also of his mother. I am reminded of the last lines of John O'Donohue's poem of the nativity: 'Outside each other now, she sees him first. Flesh of her flesh, her dreamt son on earth.'[3] Every mother who holds her first-born child could relate to that. But for Mary it must have evoked particular concerns. How could she and Joseph provide security for their new-born son? She was far away from her own family, who would have supported them, especially in the first few weeks of her baby's life. Living under foreign occupation brought hardships then as it does now to many people all over the world.

The seriousness of Mary's face touches me. She looks so young, yet the inner peace of maturity seems to radiate from her. Or is it reflected from the baby so peacefully asleep on her lap? Her child has indeed arrived safely and, for the moment, she can hold him and silently adore him. That present moment is in fact the gift and the fulfilment of God's promise to his chosen people, that the Messiah would be born within Judaism. Mary had accepted God's plan unconditionally. This presents challenges, because my acceptance of God's plans for me is often marred by my inner fears and lack of trust in him. Yet I too have experienced moments when I knew that God was close to me. Such moments are indeed gifts. In fact they are priceless and far beyond the value of material gifts.

As I look again at Mary's eyes focused on her son, I wonder what her thoughts might be. It occurs to me that from the moment of the annunciation of the angel's message to Mary, her 'yes' was put to the test. As a Jewish woman well versed in the Scriptures, Mary would never have remotely considered that she might be asked to be the mother of the Messiah. Now, as she holds him in her arms, I see and feel the incredible impact of her 'yes'. The light of the candle shines first and foremost on the baby's face but Mary is enfolded in that light. It is a sacred moment of silent communication between Jesus and his mother. He looks so peaceful as he nestles in her arms, and though his eyes are closed and he is swaddled, the Christ child seems totally relaxed. The communication between mother and son is wordless and private.

From my position in the shadows of this scene, what does it touch in me? My first reaction is a depth of gratitude for the mystery of God's love. It is hard to take on board that I am not merely looking at a scene of profound tenderness, but that I am actually part of it. I am not just an onlooker. Here before me is Christ our Saviour, 'king of kings and lord of lords' as we sing in Handel's *Messiah*. But there is no entourage, no fanfare. The word that re-emerges is 'vulnerability'. Both Mary and her child are in a precarious situation. This is no place for a baby but, being homeless, where else can they go? From the beginning, Christ entered into the reality of vast numbers of homeless, displaced and persecuted people all over the world. Somewhere deep within me is a longing to give him and his mother a home. This is not a superficial response, but a realisation that Christ wants to make his home in me. Will the door of my heart be open? This is a challenging question. I would like to answer in the affirmative, but in all honesty I would have to own that it is sometimes only partially open. The amazing thing is that God is prepared to wait for me to truly live what I have professed by the vows I took more than forty-five years ago. I marvel at his patience and his forgiveness, when the space I have offered him in my heart has so often been limited.

At this point I am aware that there seems to be no door to the room where Jesus was born. There is no one on guard to select who may enter and who is excluded. It is a place where people can come and go freely and all are welcome. Some stay for a short while, others linger.

He who has chosen to enter our world in poverty and powerlessness is always found at the margins of society. There he is available to the outcasts of society. My thoughts lead me to those who throughout the ages have been rejected by various organisations, including their church communities, because of their colour, gender or sexuality. Doors open to others, were closed against them.

This was a reality for me in 1987 when I began to work as a volunteer at the Terrence Higgins Trust in London. I remember that fear of infection was almost tangible. HIV patients in hospitals were often isolated. Their food was left outside their rooms and those visiting them had to dress up in protective clothing including gloves. Some of the medical staff refused to treat these patients, fearing they might become infected themselves. This was long before appropriate information was given to everyone involved. In those early days we had to keep lists of undertakers, GPs and dentists who were prepared to treat people who had the virus. We also needed a list of priests who would give holy communion to patients. As I now reflect on the impact of Christ into our world, I ask myself: 'Can this fragile baby really make a difference? Can he help us to break down the barriers we ourselves have created? Will God intervene on behalf of the poor?' Even as these words form in my mind, I recall a comment made by the Jesuit writer and retreat-giver, Father Anthony de Mello. He tells of a man who remonstrated with God about the poverty and injustices experienced by so many people. 'Don't you care?' was the question he put to God. There was no immediate answer, but later it came in a brief sentence: 'I made you!' I have to remind myself of that message and acknowledge that it is also meant for me. I need to ask myself: 'What am I doing for those who live as outcasts?' I have to admit that while I may appear to have spent much of my life helping those who could clearly be identified as 'outcasts', the reality is that I have often been selective in the way I have responded to their needs. That would not be Christ's response. I am aware that this new-born child in La Tour's picture also seeks a place where he can be born in my own heart. I know that, if or when I can really provide that un-conditionally, my responses to others would also bear the mark of his unconditional love. In theory that would be my desire, but in practice I am still struggling daily to make that commitment a reality in my life.

As I look again at this scene, I am conscious of the older woman. Her quiet presence is a reminder for me that God often provides support when I least expect it.

There have been many situations in my life when that has been the case. Strengthened by that encounter I can once again resume the challenges of daily activities.

There is another aspect of this picture which touches me. It is the importance of the present moment. The wonder of the birth and the stillness of the scene allows me as the onlooker to enter into that moment, even though it is now more than 2000 years after Christ's birth. Once again I ask myself: 'What do I see and what do I feel?' As I look at the closed eyes of the baby I am aware of the silent connection between him and his mother. It is the communication of the heart. I realise once again that the heart is the powerhouse of our deepest communications with God and with each other. Here, God makes his home. But many people say that the heart can mislead us. Is it not a fact that reason can be trusted more than the heart? Reason and logic are surely safer guides in our journeys through life than allowing ourselves to be moved by the heart. My response, however, is that thought alone can also mislead us. We have been given heart and mind. We need the fusion of both. As I contemplate the fragile baby in his mother's arms, my heart aches for both of them. Outside the peacefulness of the room there are dark and menacing forces. Mary has already experienced them and, likewise, so have countless mothers who have cradled their children in a hostile environment. Many women have found in Mary a person who understands the suffering of a mother's heart.

I want to end with an excerpt from an essay written in 1931 by Edith Stein who, like me, was born in Breslau. She has been an inspiration for me, partly because her background is also Jewish. She converted to Christianity, entered Carmel, but was arrested by the Nazis and ended her life in Auschwitz. She writes:

'O wonderful exchange! The creator of mankind, by taking on a human body, imparts to us his divinity. It is for this wondrous task that the Saviour came into this world. God became a child of man, so that the human race could become children of God.'[4]

As I allow these words to take root in me, I feel drawn again to Mary holding her new-born child. I can now understand a little better the awesomeness of this moment in time. God as a totally dependent baby is not an image which makes me feel comfortable. I often need to lean on God's strength. I want him to fight my battles for me. But light is beginning to dawn. As I look at Mary and Jesus, I can glimpse something of the meaning of sacrificial love. God in Mary's arms risked everything out of his desire to recreate harmony between God and the human race. Both Jesus and Mary seem to say to each other and to the Father: 'Let what you have said be done to me.'[5] The picture depicts the powerlessness and interdependence of Mary and Jesus. Each needs the other to fulfil the divine plan for our redemption. I too want to be able to say from the depth of my heart: 'Let what you have said be done to me.' I hope I can retain these words. I take with me a deeper understanding that God needs me to fulfil his plan, not as someone who is powerful, but as one who puts her trust in the powerlessness of Love incarnate. That is why he made you and me. There is no doubt in my heart that we need him to fulfil his dream for us.

With these thoughts imprinted in me, I can see that Christmas now has a deeper meaning than before. I begin to understand that I too am involved daily in the choices between the powers of darkness and light. It is no longer appropriate for me to ask: 'What has happened to the promise of peace on earth?' I know the answer lies deep within each of us. I often want peace on my own terms, and that is also the conflict within the world at large. Edith Stein comments: 'the Son of the Eternal Father must leave the splendour of heaven because the mystery of evil has wrapped the earth in dark night.'[6]

These words are astounding. They give me great hope. As a child I was content to look forward to our yearly Christmas celebrations as an end in itself. Now, I realise that Christmas is the first step towards the fulfilment of Christ's mission on Calvary and ultimately to the glory of the resurrection. We can no longer isolate Christ's birth from his sacrificial death, but we can ask him to lead us from Bethlehem to Jerusalem.

When God comes among us, he doesn't first of all clear humanity out of the way so that he can take over; he becomes a human being. He doesn't force his way to dominate and crush; he announces his arrival in the sharp, hungry cry of a new-born baby. He changes the world not by law and threat, but by death and resurrection. The anonymous mediaeval lyric puts it unforgettably:

> *'He came all so stille*
> *Where his mother was,*
> *As dew in Aprille,*
> *That falleth on the grass.'[7]*

4

WHEN I AM WEAK

When we are stricken
And cannot bear our lives any longer,
Then a tree has something to say to us:
'Be still!'[1]

Hermann Hesse

WEAKNESS AND STRENGTH may appear to be opposites but my faith journey teaches me that this isn't always the case. For example, I once thought that embracing a religious belief was actually a sign of weakness. Fifty years on, I know that, to embark on such a journey requires spiritual and moral stamina. The ongoing trek can, in fact, result in our discovering the very source of weakness and strength.

When we look back on our lives, we often remember incidents which highlight our awareness of weakness as well as our potential for strength. As a child I was dimly aware that living and dying was a fact of life for all creatures in nature and for human beings. But my first experience of watching a tree being felled terrified me. This did not seem a natural death but a murderous attack on a defenceless creature. I felt deeply for the tree. For me the foresters were ruthless men and the tree was defenceless confronted with such might. The screeching sound of the saw and the sharp blows of the axe embedded themselves in me. Worst of all was the sight of the mighty tree crashing to the ground. There was a moment of silence before the foresters completed their work, hacking off branches and sawing the trunk into several pieces. It seemed like a brutal homicide, filling me with fear, anger and a sense of helplessness. There were many echoes of this scene in my later life, when I experienced ruthlessness and arbitrary attacks on individuals and minority groups. The searing sound of the tree crashing to the ground often reverberated in my consciousness. But I came to sense that the tree I thought had been so brutally destroyed had not ended its existence. Many fir trees are felled and transformed into beautiful pine furniture. The pine wood desk in my room reminds me of that. So even in the natural world, there are signs of rebirth and resurrection. Such revelations led me to conclude that our moments of fear and helplessness can be transformed in our quest to find meaning in our lives. Once we undertake such a journey we are likely to find God walking with us.

I would like to honour three people who have taught me to gain a deeper understanding of the paradox of strength and weakness. They have touched my life at different times and places. Their own life journeys have inspired me to 'put out into deep water.'[2] Let me introduce you to Jill.

I met Jill after she had been diagnosed with

HIV/AIDS. She was a young woman and a gifted artist. On one occasion, when I visited her in hospital, she was in a side room. The wall opposite her bed was covered with her paintings and sketches. They transformed the room into a vibrant art gallery. As I entered, all was still. Jill was drowsy. John, her father, was sitting silently by her bed. After a while, John turned towards me and in painful anger said: 'It's all very well for you, Eva, you have faith. I have none.' His anguish was almost tangible. There was nothing meaningful I could utter, but I felt deeply for him. I too had often been at screaming point when God seemed absent and irrelevant. I could resonate with John's pain. It was Jill who broke the silence. She opened her eyes and turned towards her father saying: 'Dad, I don't have faith either, but I have hope.' The darkness of fear had been dispelled by the weakest person in the room. There was a long silence before her father said quietly: 'Perhaps my lack of faith is the ground for hope.' This paradox of weakness and strength remains a poignant memory for me. At times when my own faith wavers, I return to this scene and relive the power of strength Jill released for us. There is a mystery in this experience which I want to explore further.

I often wonder what enabled Jill to live 'in hope'. In the support sessions I had with her and her family, we rarely talked about spiritual matters. But as an artist Jill was, I think, in touch with the wonders of creation. For many of us, the beauties of nature evoke deep responses which open us to the great mystery of living and dying. We may not be able to put that into words, but allowing ourselves to be touched by the wordless wonders of nature can lead us into the depths of our being. For instance, watching a spectacular sunset can evoke profound feelings of amazement. I think such powerful phenomena can prepare us for the seeds of faith and hope which often lie dormant within us. I remember watching such a sunset a few years ago. It was stunning and silencing. It deepened my awareness that as the sun was going down and darkness enveloped us, the sun was actually rising on another part of our planet, heralding a new day. It was a reminder that endings and beginnings are linked to the cycle of living and dying. Such a discovery is rooted in the gifts of faith and hope. They complement each other. Both are nourished by love. This can enable us to remain close to those who have passed through death into the mystery of life eternal. But it has to be said that each person's journey of hope and faith is unique and unfolds in different ways and at different times and in many different circumstances. Jill herself would never have realised that from her position of weakness. She empowered us to move forward with hope, even at a time when her family were facing the reality that Jill would not be with them much longer.

The second person whose life has touched me deeply is my aunt Hertha who lived in Berlin. We never met in my childhood, but she came to see me when I was a novice in my congregation. Hertha was a remarkable woman with an extraordinary history. She studied engineering and gained a degree – unusual for a woman in the early part of the twentieth century. She had a promising future ahead of her, but Hitler put an end to any dreams Hertha might have had of being a pioneer in the field of engineering. Being Jewish, albeit nominally, she was arrested and deported to a concentration camp.

Ironically she was forced to design and build further extensions to the camp. I dare not imagine what it may have meant for her, for example, to design enlargements of the existing gas chambers. Hertha shared an over-crowded shed with other women. Food was scarce, too. She was often interrogated for hours and beaten during that time. But she discovered two rays of hope. The first one was symbolised by a small piece of bread. She would find this on her bunk when she returned from long and painful interrogations. She would be physically and mentally shattered, but the morsel of bread was a most powerful sign of love. It would not be an exaggeration to say that it was a sacrificial offering. All the women had meagre rations which barely kept them alive; yet they shared what they had with one another. For Hertha it was not the size of the gift, but the love with which it was offered that was life giving. When I first heard this story I was deeply moved. I felt that this was in the realm of a eucharistic offering. Christ makes himself known to us in diverse ways.

Hertha's second sign of hope was rooted outside the camp. It was a young cherry tree which stood in a field beyond the barbed wire. She saw it blossom every year in the camp. This gave her hope and a reason to live through the stark winter months: she wanted to see it again to draw strength from its fragile beauty. 'I had no belief in God when I was arrested and taken to the camp, but when I was liberated I left, knowing that God exists even amongst the evil within the camp and on the other side of the barbed wire fence,' she once told me. The tree had conveyed this to her. She clung to that faith. I don't know if she ever explored it further or if this was sufficient for her. God alone knows how and when to lead each of us to the fulfilment of faith. Many people who have suffered gruesome persecution cannot bring themselves to be in membership with any institution even when it is benign. It is a sad fact of life – and part of our human frailty – that even the best of religious institutions have their dark components. But Hertha's three years in a concentration camp enabled her to know that the love of God is greater than the evil of humankind.

After her liberation, Hertha was given the opportunity to live in Sweden. She often recalled her experience of leaving Germany, in the company of many other women. They were promised food packets for the journey, but the organiser of this trip, a Swedish nobleman, asked the helpers to give each of them an extra packet before handing out the food. 'The contents of these packets are just as essential to these women,' he remarked. He was right. Each delighted woman was given a vanity bag, containing make-up, scent, and a mirror. Hertha said that this man's sensitivity had touched all of them deeply. They needed both parcels – but the order in which they were presented was important. The vanity bags were a sign that they would be able to reclaim their femininity. The thoughtfulness of this man was as much a life-saver as the food parcels – helping the women to take their first steps in moving from weakness to strength.

After a short time in Sweden, Hertha emigrated to the United States. Ironically she returned to Germany for short periods, as that was the only country that could offer her treatment for the muscle damage she had sustained through the beatings. It was a cathartic experience for her – and perhaps for those treating her arms. All of us can experience personal as well as communal guilt. Hertha's presence in the clinic may well have enabled the staff there to allow themselves to be healed from the burden of guilt which many German people of the older generation carry even to this day. Everyone she met at the clinic showed her love and respect. I think that Hertha herself was aware that a mutual healing process was taking place. Strength and weakness were deeply entwined.

Personally, I feel very blessed to have met Hertha. Her zest for life was infectious. When she settled in the States, she loved entertaining and was usually the life and soul of the parties she organised or attended. My brother, who also emigrated to the States, got to know her well and that was a blessing for both of them. When we all met at Mayfield during my noviciate year, before taking vows, we represented a variety of faith journeys. My mother and sister were members of the Church of England, my brother was a hopeful agnostic but a deeply spiritual person, and I was a Roman Catholic. Hertha was a freed spirit, cherished by God as she was in her own uniqueness. God's own loving respect for each individual is likewise an illustration of the paradox of strength and weakness. To allow people to grow spiritually at their own pace is not a sign of weakness but, on the contrary, an indication of strength. God believes in our potential long before we recognise it ourselves. He both protects and nurtures our seeds of faith.

The third person to leave a deep impression on my faith is connected with a recent expedition to one of the L'Arche communities in Britain for a week of guided prayer among the developmentally disabled. I have always had a profound respect for L'Arche's founder, Jean Vanier. Although I have been involved in the retreat movement in England and abroad for the past twenty years, I have never been so moved and so appropriately humbled as I was during the week at L'Arche, in February 2005.

The prayer companions were invited to three sessions in preparation for our meetings with the 'pilgrims'. I was only able to go to two meetings, but was immediately touched by the sensitive way we were led to prepare for this event. Some had taken part in similar weeks of guided prayer; others were as new to it as I was. Initially when I heard we had to be at three preparatory meetings, I wondered why this was necessary. Surely all of us were already experienced in this field. Within an hour of our first meeting I realised the arrogance of such a standpoint. In retrospect, I feel that God or my angel gave me a push in the right direction. I realised that regardless of my past experiences, this week would challenge me to empty myself to receive a gift from God who makes 'the whole of creation new'.[3] I needed to lay aside the temptation to be in control. This confronted me with my own sense of vulnerability and weakness which at the outset was not easy to own but, once the retreat started, it gave me a deep feeling of freedom, knowing that within that framework of weakness I could find new strength and joy.

I was asked to accompany two 'pilgrims': a volunteer worker and one of the residents, Peter, a young, good-looking black man who had taken part in a similar week of guided prayer and asked to do it again. As he had a hearing problem I was advised to ensure that he had his aid switched on. Peter can speak, but his words flow like a torrent. I found it difficult to understand him. That presented no problems because there were other ways of communicating with each other. From the moment we met, I felt that Peter 'spoke' through his eyes, his hands and his body movement. It made me realise how much we miss when we rely predominantly on verbal skills as the norm for communication. Peter liked the flowers on a small table which became our focal point. We talked about the loveliness of the daffodils, all at different stages of unfolding. Likewise a pot of three hyacinths, whose colour only showed towards the end of the week. I brought some mustard and cress seeds, and asked Peter if he would like to plant them, so that we might see them grow. He took them into his hands and carefully arranged them on damp paper. He distributed them gently, slowly and with great reverence. We covered them so that they could grow in the darkness. Each day, when Peter came for his session, he looked at the seeds and was amazed how quickly they were growing. We praised God for all these beautiful things and for our time together. Peter enjoyed singing hymns. He knew 'Peace is flowing like a river', so we sang two verses at the beginning and end of our sessions.

At our next meeting I showed him some simple pictures made with melted wax, using a variety of colours and a miniature iron. I asked if he would like to create some patterns himself. He seemed eager. He chose his own colours and allowed them to melt on the base of the heated iron which I held for him. I showed him how to use the iron to 'paint' his first picture. He was excited when he discovered the lovely shapes he had created.

During the third session he held the iron himself and applied the colours he wanted to use. He allowed me to place my hand loosely on his to guide the iron in various ways. I was surprised that he had that degree of trust. In our prayer we thanked God for allowing us to be co-creators with him and showing us his gifts hidden within us. I think that the seeds, the flowers and the painting were important for Peter. He also brought something of his own to the last session. It was a scrapbook with pictures of a holiday in Florida. I had been told that he had swam with dolphins. He was excited to show me the photographs and his own paintings in the book. Although I could not understand his words, I gleaned a lot from his intonation and the obvious pride he had in showing me the diary.

For me, this was a new experience of prayer guiding. Peter enabled me to let go of my familiar responses with retreatants. I had to admit to myself how I often like to be in control, especially when I am unsure of myself. My own journey of learning to trust the love and guidance of the Holy Spirit continues daily. During that week, I was definitely not in control. Surprisingly, it was a great relief to be aware of that and to be able to acknowledge it. In accompanying Peter on his spiritual journey, I felt that it was indeed I who was weak and Peter who was strong. There was no doubt that it was Peter who showed me how to communicate with him and it was the invisible presence of the Holy Spirit who guided both of us.

On the last day when all of us met for the final celebration in a nearby church, Peter indicated that he wanted to show me something before the service began. He led me to a set of drums. I imagined that they were probably used in various liturgies. I had been told that he played drums. He sat down and gave me an impromptu performance. No one objected to the sounds he invoked. Initially he played softly and wistfully; then, using the foot pedal, filled the church with extraordinary sounds, rhythm and changes of moods. I felt that he was communicating something about his own feelings: his joy and his sadness, his anger and his serenity. His skill and sensitivity to various tones and combinations of sounds evoked a deep response in me. I felt that Peter wanted to give me something. I accepted it with joy and gratitude.

In our consumer society disabled people are not always valued on the same level as others. They are deemed to be different, and often looked on as inferior. What I experienced in my brief week at L'Arche was another value system. The quality of love, trust and concern for one another was visible at all times. Each person was treated with genuine respect and with deep understanding. It will take time to internalise such a rich experience. It provides me with much food for thought about what it means to be a follower of Christ. If I have gleaned something about the weakness and strength of such discipleship, it is Peter who has enabled me to do so.

Jill, Hertha and Peter have never met. But together they lie firmly rooted in my heart. In different ways each has shown that our inner weaknesses can be transformed into strength. We need mutual support to find this and may discover it in unexpected places and at unexpected times. Retreats and weeks of guided prayer enable us to embark upon and deepen our spiritual journeys. For every person that journey is unique. Perhaps the first step lies in our desire to begin. It could be the most important journey of our lives.

I asked the tree
Speak to me of God
And it blossomed.[4]

5

TRANSFORMATION

For me trees have always been the most penetrating teachers.[1]

Hermann Hesse

EVERY YEAR I make several visits to friends who live in a remote part of Wales. I usually start my journey early in the morning and aim to arrive in time for lunch. I am keen to get there, but I don't hurry. That's an agreement I have made with myself. I want to have space to savour the drive and the luxury of being away from the phone and the pollution, noise and bustle of central London. But as I head towards the Forest of Dean, it's hard to keep the speed down. Once I have reached the forest, it beckons me to stop and rest a while. There is a pervading sense of God's presence: 'Pause a while and know that I am God.'[2] I find one of my favourite parking places and turn off the engine. It's a sacred moment when I can breathe in the scent of the forest, let go of the city tensions and listen to different sounds. In the winter there is a particular silence. The trees are bare and the ground is hard but not for ever. Well below the surface there are stirrings. This resonates with the transformation from my inner struggles of darkness into the light of faith.

Each season provides images which echo different stages of my faith journey. Springtime is magical with bluebells and wood anemones carpeting the ground. It is a reminder that these fragile wild flowers have a hidden strength which enables them to fulfil their destiny. I have to search for that within myself, too. In summer I listen to the birds, and watch for those species which we no longer see in our polluted cities. It is a time to reflect quietly on the process of transformation and to give thanks for the growth that has taken place. In the autumn I revel in the feast of colours: the richness of the gold, green, copper leaves carpeting the ground below. This reminds me that each season has a specific task in the life cycle of nature. I can echo that in the ongoing cycle of my spiritual maturing. I have to let go of many things I am attached to – just as a tree has to let go of its autumn glory and prepare for the vulnerability of winter. The nakedness of the trees in winter, the hardness of the earth and the limited amount of daylight are reminders of the barren periods in my life. But there is always hope that a new season is already potentially at work. I cannot see what is happening below the hard surface, but the cycle of the seasons encourages me to wait in faith. It never ceases to amaze me that even in the eightieth year of my life, my faith can still be greened. That seems a healthy awareness. With this pattern in mind, I want to trace the seasons of my faith journey and hope that this may also resonate with your own unique growth in faith.

People have often asked me: 'Why or how did you become a Catholic?' For many years I found this a difficult question to answer. I did not want to give the impression that I was avoiding a meaningful reply, yet I could not verbalise the gift of faith. My conversion to Roman Catholicism was as much a surprise to me as it was to my family and friends. I am aware now that seeds of faith were sown very early in my life, but remained deep within me until the time when they began to germinate. This is nature's way and often the pattern of our spiritual journeys. 'There is a season for everything ... '[3]

My earliest awareness of faith dates to an experience I had when I was six. I had been ill for many weeks with jaundice and the doctor recommended that I should spend some time at a convalescent home for children. I have only one specific memory of that experience. Each night when we were put to bed, one of the staff would kneel down by our bedside and pray the Lord's Prayer with us. That was a new experience for me, a Jewish girl. When I returned home, I told my mother that this was a proper way to end each day. I taught her the words and showed her where to kneel by my bed. The fact that my mother was willing to do so is more amazing to me now than it would have been then. I think we continued the ritual for several weeks and then it gradually faded out. But it must have remained deep within me for nearly two decades.

Another meaningful faith experience occurred on a visit to my cousin's family. They, too, were Jewish and celebrated the traditional feast days. I was there during a school holiday and took part in the celebration of Pesach (Passover). The ritual fascinated me, even though

I had no knowledge of Hebrew. Perhaps it was an experience that prompted me to start searching for my own spiritual roots, even without knowing it.

Apart from these two experiences in my early childhood, I had no conscious awareness that God existed. It was only when I came to England in 1939, as a refugee on one of the children's transports, that I had further direct contact with Christianity. I was fostered by a Christian couple called Mr and Mrs Finton who lived in Oxford. They had a 21-year-old son, Michael, who met me at Liverpool Street station. It was only much later that I discovered that Mr and Mrs Finton had a daughter, who had died when she was about my age. When they saw my photo, which was attached to our application forms for emigration, they chose me, as I had fair, curly hair like their daughter. They hoped I could be a replacement for her.

Mr Finton was a headmaster at a local primary school. I was told to call him Uncle Bob. He was a kind person who left the running of the house and other major decisions to Aunt Edna, his wife. This was very different to the structure in my own family. I never really took to Aunt Edna – partly because her teeth stuck out! I disliked being kissed by her. She was tall, rounded, and an imposing figure with hair swept back in a bun. Her word was law. I learnt that especially every Sunday, when we dressed up in our 'Sunday best' – hat and all – in order to go to church. I found this boring. It did not endear me to a God who apparently required this weekly ritual.

I only knew very few English words when I arrived. This also complicated our relationships during the first few weeks. Once I started school, I was soon able to converse in English.

As I think back to those days, I realise it must also have been a difficult time for the Fintons. In their own way, they tried their best to help me to settle down. I was taken out in their car, each weekend. I remember Aunt Edna being cross with me, because I often curled up in the back seat, instead of looking at the beautiful countryside. I was told I was ungrateful. The fact was that I was homesick and longing to be back in familiar surroundings. At that stage I had no idea that I might be reunited with my family.

My placement with the Fintons broke down within a year of my arrival. By this time, my parents had come to England on a visiting visa, but war was declared while they were here, so they had to stay in Oxford. As refugees, they had no home of their own. My mother worked as a resident cook in a large household; my father lived in a small bed-sitting room. His relationship with the Fintons was acrimonious. This led them to give us an ultimatum: either they would adopt me as their daughter, or I would have to leave them. My mother explained this situation to me and asked me to make the decision. That was a difficult task for a 12-year-old girl. The Fintons could offer me material security, but blood is thicker than water and I chose to stay with my mother. I was given a small attic room close to hers. These were difficult times for all of us.

It is not surprising, I think, that I experienced periods of depression as well as a deep-seated anger. I longed to have the security of a family with our own home and garden. The uprooting from Germany to England was more complex than I could ever have envisaged. At the time there was no one with whom I could share these powerful feelings. I felt I was under pressure to be 'good and grateful' to those who were trying to help me. But I could not express my anguish. I learnt to keep my thoughts to myself. That was costly but I have no regrets. It was precisely such experiences which enabled me throughout my professional life to reach out to those who are on the edge of our social, educational and spiritual structures.

My school days in Oxford were marked by my failures in exams as well as my refusal to 'play the game' – whether on a hockey field or in other areas of my life. Not having been brought up in an educational system which includes daily games periods, I could not see the sense of running up and down a field, clutching a stick and – in my case – aiming to avoid any contact with a ball! Always the last one to be chosen for a team, it was as painful for me as for the team I had to join. It did nothing to enhance my battered confidence.

As I relive those years, I see them as a long winter period with relatively little light. There were inner storms and outer ones too. These months were not the peaceful winter scenes of white snow which transforms a countryside into a fairyland. Emotionally, they were an experience of cold hunger and a longing for the warmth of sunlight which would revitalise the earth and me.

Then one day I was given the opportunity to go to a boarding school. I welcomed this. It felt as though I might come to life again. The hope of spring was in the air.

This school was unusual. Team games had little space on the timetable. Instead we were actively involved in running the farm attached to the school. My first task was to learn how to feed calves who had been weaned. I was taught to do so by Elizabeth, one of the senior girls. It was the very best kind of 'therapy' I could have had. I can still recall the feeling of the little calf's rough tongue sucking on my fingers in the pail of warmed milk. I bonded with this creature who was going through a weaning process. My deep love of animals and nature found an affinity with this environment. Its spiritual ethos also touched me. The headmistress, Miss Laycock, foundress of this unusual school, was a Quaker. It was here that I first experienced the value and power of silence. Each day after we had finished our studies, a bell rang. The entire school kept five minutes' silence wherever we were at that moment. At the second sounding of the bell, we filed into a large room where Miss Laycock read or spoke to us for a few minutes before we had our evening meal. I remember these experiences as being peaceful, and challenging. The short periods of silence were rarely broken and when they were it was usually by a new student. Little did I know at that time that Elizabeth and I would meet again fourteen years later, when I became a novice in the same religious order she had entered two years earlier. With hindsight, how could I ever doubt God's invisible presence?

Although I was emotionally revitalised at this school, my academic achievements were fragmentary. I left having failed to achieve the pass mark in five subjects required to gain a leaving certificate. Most other pupils continued their studies at universities. I applied for a two-year residential course for nursery nurses and passed those exams with credit and distinction! This restored some of my confidence and led me to think that I needed to re-sit my school exams.

I did so during a year when I worked as an au pair for a family with three lively children. I loved the work and enjoyed the studies, but at a deeper level was again doubtful that I would pass my exams. Depression set in once more. This time I found myself shouting inwardly: 'If there is a God, show me!' There appeared to be no answer. I bargained with the unseen God, planning to take my life if I did not pass the exams. This was not a vain scream for help nor a dramatic attention-seeking gesture. I saw it as the only logical response to yet another academic failure. The week leading up to re-sits was fraught because the family I worked for went on holiday and I was left homeless. They had assumed that I would come with them, but failed to understand how important it was for me to take the exams. I spent most of my meagre savings on paying for bed and breakfast accommodation. My daily diet consisted of a pint of milk, cereal and sandwiches. I was seething with anger and frustration. If God existed was this the way he dealt with his followers? It was only many years later, that I realised that God had not abandoned me nor was he offended by my anger. I passed the exams and was successful in gaining a place on a teacher training course at Homerton College, Cambridge.

The next three years were an unfolding of springtime. I felt that I could grow again. I sowed my wild oats in several fields. I had a steady boyfriend and enjoyed the social life of the university, including May Balls, punting on the river and climbing back into college over a stone wall long after curfew. But the most significant change was the urge I felt to discover more about God. I realised that the God I challenged had not punished me for it. I was dimly aware that he was waiting for me to find him. Thus began a long trek of spiritual searching. While I was at Cambridge, I explored a seemingly endless number of religious groups. They varied from the most traditional to the latest vogue in charismatic spirituality. Each one was welcoming but I was reluctant to be caught in their net. The formality of earnest students in the Bible reading groups bored me. Nor did I feel I could belong to the other end of the spectrum amidst the 'happy clapping' and clashing of cymbals group. In fact I did not feel at home in any of them. But I did believe that God was with me in this journey of exploration. I learned a truth which has never left me: God is a God who waits. He is neither a dictator nor a Victorian father. God believed in me long before I could believe in him. In retrospect this was a time when I felt that faith was surfacing. Spring was not only in the air, but I began to be aware that there was an inner movement of new life within me. We need to cherish such moments. That is why it is so important for me to break my journey when I drive to Wales. The Forest of Dean is a momentary resting place to reconnect with the seasons of my spiritual journey and to give thanks.

During this period of my life I met Stella, who was considerably older than I was. She was petite and dressed in long flowing skirts, wore unusual jewellery and had a drawer full of delightful silk scarves. Stella taught drama and had other creative gifts. She wrote poetry and owned a gypsy caravan, which stood in an orchard on a farm, overlooking the Chiltern Hills. We spent many weekends and holidays there. She was a committed Catholic and we had long, deep conversations about the existence of God. Stella was a patient listener. She shared my love of nature and also introduced me to the Gospel of John. Gradually light dawned and I recognised in Jesus the God who became man. We explored the writings of the prophet Isaiah and I began to resonate with the Hebrew Scriptures. I grew to love the Psalms. The opening words of Psalm 139 touched me deeply and have remained with me throughout the years: 'Yahweh, you examine me and know me.'[4] When I reflected on these words, it amazed me that God knew me in the depth of my being and yet, despite my many failings, had not abandoned me. Apparently he knew me before I was born. 'I have called you by your name, you are mine.'[5] That was mind-blowing and yet consoling. He knew me better than I knew myself. This was an image of a father totally different from the experience I had in my relationship with my own father. Seemingly God's love for me was unconditional. God believed in me! Slowly and falteringly, I began to believe in myself.

Through my long conversations with Stella and our exploration of St John's gospel, selected psalms, as well as more contemporary writings, I began to respond to God's love for me in a personal way. The stumbling block was that I did not feel drawn to any organised religious group. I felt happiest when I could praise God in all the aspects of nature. I could resonate with storms as well as with peaceful pastures. My love of trees continued to give me space to meditate. I wanted to be a free spirit in my praise of God. As I think about this now, I can see that my negative experiences of powerful organisations made me wary of aligning myself to any particular Christian group. However, my discussions with Stella and my reading about the history and development of Christianity drew me to Catholicism. It always makes me smile when I think about that. For one who had reservations about hierarchical structures, Roman Catholicism might seem an unlikely choice.

So what drew me towards Rome in my early twenties? I think there were two factors. The first is that my sister had been baptised in the Church of England and shortly after this, my mother followed. At that stage I remember thinking – with the arrogance of youth and an air of superiority – 'nothing will ever get me to clutch the straw of institutional religion.' Secondly, I felt that the history of the Catholic Church was so studded with human failure and sinfulness that there might be room for me there. God must surely be there, I thought, for the frail human structure to have survived the test of time. The sexual, political and financial sins as well as all the different facets of human power struggles, are part of the continuous life struggle of the Church – open for all to see. The Church was not a club for nice people. There was room for me there.

When I told my mother and sister that I had chosen to become a Catholic my mother's shocked reply was: 'Why do you always have to be different?' Initially it was a painful situation for each of us. In later years, far from dividing our family bonds, it actually united us. We began to realise that unity is not achieved by uni-formity and that there can be a richness in diversity. Many Christians hoped that the changes proposed by the second Vatican council would enable us to move closer together. However, wounds of division still remain and these are painful for us. The Church moves slowly, but at least it is not static.

I was confirmed shortly after my baptism. The

uniqueness of my friendship with Stella deepened as both of us could delight in the wonders of our spiritual journeys. We shared a flat together and delighted in each other's company. I think the next five years were the most peaceful ones of my life. I was aware that the roots of my faith were being strengthened. It seemed like a prolonged summer time. I remember particularly our relaxing weekends at Stella's caravan: the spectacle of early sunrises and late sunsets. The beauty of outer lights echoed my joy of the growth of the inner light of faith. But that was not to last for ever. Deep within me there were stirrings of new growth, which both frightened and attracted me. I wanted to find a meaningful way of thanking God for the gift of faith and responding to his sacrificial love.

One of my dreams in my early twenties was to marry and have six children. We would live on a remote island in Scotland and farm the land! Gradually I realised that God's plans for me were different. I did not want to recognise this. However, the seeds were sown and they sprouted. I realised that the initial call to become a Christian was now being followed by a deepening of that vocation to take vows as a religious sister. The sacrifice involved in this was a profound shock. I really did not want to own this call. I dreaded the consequences of such a step, particularly for my mother and sister, and for Stella. I knew how painful it would be for each of them – and of course for myself. Stella had always been aware that this might be God's will and I realised she would not want to block my way. Once again we entered into deep conversation and prayed to be given some direction to indicate the path we needed to follow.

Several years earlier Stella had been a lecturer at a Catholic teacher training college, led by sisters of the Society of the Holy Child Jesus. It was an educational order founded in 1846 by an American woman, Cornelia Connelly. Stella suggested that I might like to meet one of the sisters, to talk about the uncertainties regarding my future. At that point I was not ready to do so. The matter was left in abeyance, but it would not go away.

Eventually, Stella said jokingly: 'I dare you to meet Mother Mary Fidelis.' The meeting took place the following week. The caricature I had built up of this sister was shattered in the first few moments, when she offered me tea and cakes.

We met several times and I was impressed by her enthusiasm and interest in a wide range of educational matters. She lent me a book on the life of Cornelia Connelly. I was amazed by this woman's story. In short, I realised that the next step in my own spiritual journey was to ask to be admitted as a postulant in the Society. When I broke this news to my mother, she agonised: 'How can I tell this to my friends?' I realised that this decision was much harder for her to bear than my becoming a Catholic had been. It took a long time for her to come to terms with this seemingly 'unnatural way of life'. She wondered where she had failed me in my decision 'to run away from life'. I realised too that she had hoped I would marry. She would have loved to have been a grandmother to my children. Yet in later years, she told her friends that becoming a nun had been 'the making of Eva!'

Predictably, my noviciate years were something of a rollercoaster. During the first year I was very uncertain if I would stay the course. There were many moments when I told myself 'next week I'll leave.' In the second year I was often afraid that I might be told to leave. Community life was not easy. That is still the case. But I know now that we are given the grace needed to clear the many hurdles which confront us day by day. I have no doubts now that my vocation in life is rooted in the Society of the Holy Child Jesus. During difficult moments, I have been encouraged by the spiritual journey of Cornelia Connelly, our foundress. One of her sayings has often supported me: 'I am a cosmopolitan, I live in this world and heaven is my home.' I can identify with that statement. It gives me hope and encourages me to live in the present and look towards the future.

Leaving Stella was undoubtedly the most painful part of my decision to enter religious life. This was a truly sacrificial experience for both of us. We felt that our relationship was God's unsolicited gift to us. It was life giving and fulfilling. The thought of separation called for faith and trust in God such as I had not previously experienced. In time, we realised that each of us had been given the strength to accept this in the mystery of God's plans. But this did not alleviate the pain, especially during the years of my noviciate. In later years, we were able to rebuild our relationship, albeit in a different form. Externally, we were restricted to limited time together and initially that was painful for both of us. But internally the bond between us did not diminish. Both of us recognised that the gift of love was deeply rooted. In a mysterious way, our separation was not death dealing, but life giving – for ourselves and others.

I was able to visit Stella frequently when she was in a home for the elderly. She was serene and waiting to 'go home'. Her prayer during the last stages of her life was 'Maranatha – come, Lord Jesus.' Sadly, my last visit to her was when she was in a coma, but I felt that she knew I was by her bedside. She was at peace.

Stella's death has made me aware that our faith journeys are not diminished by death. The same is true of other significant people who have died. Of course there is the pain of separation. But there is also the sense that 'in my end is my beginning'.[6] For me the death of important people in my life – for instance, my mother's death – is now an autumn experience. It is a time to gather the fruits of a lifetime and store them deep in my heart. That becomes our meeting place. It may shock some, but I would include in that gathering 'all creatures who on earth do dwell', such as a faithful dog or other pets who played significant parts in our lives.

When I reflect on my past life, I often think of it as a patchwork blanket made of different textures, colours and patterns. It is still unfinished. The time has not yet come when I will sit in an armchair with the blanket over my knees. God is still calling me to 'get up and go!' I am looking forward to my next drive through the Forest of Dean.

I have a dream too, that one day we shall walk this earth as if it were a new world – and in that time it will be new, for we shall see it for ourselves with new eyes and touch each other with a new and gentle spirit. We will know the delight of the sacred within us and the joy of being partners, co-creators with the earth and with God.[7]

6

HEALING BROKENNESS

When a tree is cut down
And reveals its naked death wound to the sun
One can read its whole history
In the luminous inscribed disc of its trunk.[1]

Hermann Hesse

THIS QUOTATION highlights the vulnerability we experience when we try to name the pain of brokenness in our lives. It speaks to us of the reality of our own death wounds. At different stages of our earthly journeys we can discover several cycles of living and dying. But there is life after death for us. And for trees. The timber trade witnesses to that.

I have always loved wooden furniture: the rich smoothness of a mahogany table, the solidity of oak bookshelves or the glow of rosewood on the casing of musical instruments. But I have a particular liking for simple pine tree furniture because it openly displays its wounds by the scars embedded in the wood. These become visible when a tree is felled and its outer bark is removed.

As human beings we inflict hurts on others and on ourselves. We bear many wounds and scars, but we tend to hide them from view. The experience of our woundedness is often rooted in our past, inherited or internalised from early childhood onwards. Unlike trees, we are able to reflect on the hurts we receive as well as those we impose on others. We also have the power to offer and accept forgiveness. But where is God in this process?

In the 1980s I had the opportunity of returning to Germany to attend a Jewish/Christian study week near Koblenz. When I arrived, I had time to explore the town. It felt strange to be in the country of my birth again. What surprised me most were the inner feelings this evoked. I looked at men and women who were older than I was and wondered: 'Were you one of them – a member of Hitler's Nazi party?' Shocked by the intensity of fear and anger this evoked in me, it was difficult to know how to process such deep-rooted hatred. It was a frightening experience.

When our course began, the following morning, I took part in a small discussion group. We were asked to introduce ourselves and say briefly where we were from. When it was my turn, I mentioned the fact that this was my first return to Germany since I had left as a Jewish refugee in 1939. Suddenly, an elderly man opposite me appeared to be taken unwell. He looked pale and worried. Later, he asked me if we could meet and have some time to talk. We agreed to do so after lunch.

It was a beautiful afternoon. Snow had fallen during

the night and ours were the first footsteps on the path. We walked through pine trees decked in snow, sparkling in sunlight. Thomas explained that he had been deeply shocked when he had heard that I came from Jewish/German roots. He told me his story. A retired doctor and a devout Catholic, he had hoped that he would never be forced to join the Nazi party. But shortly before the war ended, it was made clear to him that if he did not become a party member, he and his family would suffer. His daughters would not be allowed to go to university, the family would be socially ostracised and he could be arrested. The implications were ominous so he reluctantly signed up.

When the war ended and the allies moved in, he was commandeered by the occupation army to work in a concentration camp ministering to those who were still alive. What he saw shattered him. There were insufficient medical supplies to help survivors in their pitiful state. It was a nightmare experience for Thomas, especially as he, like many Germans, was unaware of the horrors that eventually confronted him in the camp. As a man of deep faith, he was particularly distressed. He felt he had allowed himself to collude with the Nazis and was therefore partly responsible for the unimaginable suffering around him. As a result, he had a breakdown.

He never completely recovered. That day, sitting opposite me, had brought his pain to the surface again. He wondered if he could ever be forgiven for his collusion with the Nazis. As I listened, I became aware of the hatred I had felt towards some of the men and women in Koblenz. I realised how unjust that was. Thomas made me aware that not every person who joined the Nazi party did so out of admiration for Hitler. As we shared our stories, we felt released from the fears within us. We embraced and wept, asking each other's forgiveness. It was an extraordinary process of mutual healing. Both of us were aware that this was happening not only for ourselves, but also for others whose lives we would touch. Standing in the sunlit snow we experienced a closeness with Christ 'who makes all things new'. Whenever I recall that encounter these words and the following verses from a vision of St John, recorded in the Book of Revelation, come to mind:

'You see this city? Here God lives among men. He will make his home among them; they shall be his people, and he will be their God; his name is God-with-them. He will wipe away all tears from their eyes; there will be no more death, and no more mourning or sadness. The world of the past has gone.'[2]

There is no doubt that this gift of inner healing was intended for Thomas and me. Both of us experienced the healing power of God's love which transformed our feelings of fear, anger and self-hatred. Whenever that happens, we can be released from our burden of guilt and can then reach out to others with renewed strength.

As I recall this experience, I am aware that our sense of time is quite different from God's timing. God has infinite thoughts compared to our limited horizons. The healing for Thomas and me was well timed. Part of the process was the encouragement each of us could offer to the other. Left to oneself, it is all too easy to become despondent. As I grow older, I catch glimpses of God's wisdom and love, where previously I might not have noticed them. It is precisely because God knows our strengths and weaknesses that he does not despair of us.

I am no longer afraid of failing, because I know that each failure can be transformed.

We may have to delve deep within the labyrinth of our inner being to allow past wounds to surface and be healed. We need to acknowledge that they are there and bring them into the light of day. That is what Thomas and I were led to do. Through listening to each other, we could name our own failures and experience compassion for each other. What touches me repeatedly is that it was in such a stunning setting that we were called to reveal God's love to each other. Twenty-four hours earlier, neither of us knew that the other existed. Sceptics may well say that our meeting was a coincidence. But I have since learnt to recognise God through incidents in my own and other people's lives. When that happens, our inner darkness can be transformed by the light of God's redemptive love.

The meeting with Thomas was a daylight event. But inner healing can also take place through the darkness of night, when we are asleep. Dreams have long been recognised as powerful forms of communication. They can shed light on past hurts and unlock us from the grip of fear. Throughout my early years, I was troubled by the negative feelings I felt towards my father. I thought of him as a powerful tyrant whose every word had to be obeyed. As I did not live up to his expectations, I often experienced the heaviness of his hand. I feared him. As soon as I was independent, I decided to sever all contact with him. For years I felt guilty about this, but I also felt relieved that I had the courage to protect myself. But this did not bring me peace. And on a spiritual level, I found it difficult to relate to God as Father. I carried the burden of fear and hatred for many years. This changed unexpectedly.

One night I dreamed that my brother, Dick, came to visit me. I was delighted, as he and I were very close and his death, a few years earlier, had affected me deeply. In the dream, Dick beckoned me to follow him. He took me through a long tunnel and into a clearing. There I saw my father sitting on the ground, like a small boy, playing with a toy farm. He had his back to me. He held a small sunflower in his hand and I was given to understand that he did not know where to plant it. He gazed at it tenderly and with great sadness. Deeply moved by this vision of the powerful man I had always feared, I gradually became aware of somewhat different feelings towards him. I saw him as fragile and lonely. This touched my heart. When my brother indicated that it was time for me to leave, I was reluctant to go. But the image has remained with me and, with the passing of time, my feelings towards my father have changed radically. My only regret is that we were not able to experience this while he was alive. But I firmly believe that death is not final. I often relive that encounter with my father holding the sunflower with such sadness and tenderness. All the façade of power and might had vanished. He appeared to me like a tree which had been stripped of all its leaves, showing its vulnerability in its bare and fragile branches.

The dividing line between the living and those who have passed through death into the mystery of life is not impenetrable. I feel genuine compassion for my father now. The image of him in the dream was of a frail and isolated person. I would never have envisaged him in those terms in my younger days. But these insights touched something profound in me. Perhaps it was a recognition that he and I had more in common than I ever thought possible. It has made me realise that the road of forgiveness can be a long trek. All healing and reconciliation requires time. That is true of our visible wounds and even more so of the inner wounds which may be dormant for years. We have doctors who tend our outer wounds. But we need spiritual support to heal our invisible wounds. Albert Schweitzer, the philosopher and missionary doctor, once said: 'Most of us do not know that we carry our own doctor around inside us. We are at our best,' he said, 'when we give the doctor who resides in each of us the chance to go to work.'[3] I now interpret his words in terms of the healing power of the Holy Spirit at work within us.

The older I get, the more aware I am that there are three dimensions to the concept of forgiveness. First, to ask for forgiveness and, second, to offer it to another. The third is the most difficult one: to forgive ourselves. It takes courage to reach a point when we can begin to accept our own imperfections. But once we have recognised that and owned up to the flaws, we can make allowances for others as well as for ourselves. This was the inner gift Thomas and I experienced. The key to it was God's *compassion*, a word deeply rooted in Christian faith. I am particularly aware of it, as I am writing during the last few days of Lent, leading into Holy Week. For Christians these days recall the events of Christ's passion, death and resurrection. In this context, compassion is not just a word, but the deepest expression of love incarnate. It flows from the heart of Christ, the Son of God, to every created being. Intrinsically, compassion means suffering with and for others. Christ took upon himself the suffering and brokenness of humanity to reconcile us with God. In retrospect, I am aware that the encounter between Thomas and me helped us recognise God's compassion for each of us. That insight enabled us to have compassion for each other and for ourselves like the rising of the sun transforming the darkness of night into a new day.

If you do not have faith in a personal God, you may not feel comfortable with this image. I sympathise, because I, too, experienced doubt for many years. Faith is a gift. It cannot be manufactured. But it can be desired and hoped for. When we live with hope, our fears will decrease and faith will deepen. Faith and hope are inseparable. They operate together and sustain each other. Our faith may be no larger than a tiny seed, but it can be nurtured and helped to grow. For this to happen we need to ask for the gift of hope. I have known people to say: 'My faith is shattered, but I still hope that things might change.' They often do so.

Hope takes on different functions. This was particularly evident when I worked as a bereavement counsellor. I have spent many hours with parents and partners of people whose loved ones were close to death or had already died from AIDS-related illnesses. Bereavement does not always start after death, but often during the period when a person's life is diminishing. I experienced this when I facilitated support groups for relatives, partners and friends of people affected by HIV/AIDS. In our monthly meetings we had many poignant moments when a parent or partner could name the grief and the guilt he felt because he was unable to offer meaningful support to someone he loved dearly. The question most often raised was: 'Whose fault is it?' This was especially painful for parents of gay sons. Sometimes a father would confide that he had alienated the son by the harsh treatment he gave him when the son revealed to his parents that he was gay and diagnosed HIV-positive. Sometimes the son was told to leave the house and never to return. Subsequently the father's guilt became so deeply rooted that it seemed impossible for him to forgive himself. Within the safety of the group, feelings could be named. Fear was the most common and painful feeling. 'Where have I failed?' was a frequent question. Couples blaming each other was another issue. But because of the high level of trust and mutual compassion in the group, most members were able to be honest with themselves and begin the long journey towards becoming reconciled with their sons and learning to forgive themselves in that process. Sharing pain enables us to open our hearts. When that happens, hope begins to rise and enable people to move out of their inner darkness of guilt and self-accusations.

Facing the difficulties of forgiving ourselves, I am drawn to Peter, my favourite of Christ's disciples. He repeatedly failed to understand Christ's teaching, yet was destined to become the leader of the group. Peter's impulsiveness and his many failures were public. But he learnt from his mistakes. This was especially poignant when he declared indignantly that he would never deny Christ. Jesus forewarned him that he would indeed deny him before a cock crowed.[4] It isn't hard to imagine Peter's anguish when he heard the cry of the cock and remembered Christ's words. I feel I can identify with Peter. There have been many times in my life when I also felt too ashamed of my 'betrayals' to name and own them to myself, let alone to others and to God. Many of us have that problem, particularly if in our childhood we experienced conditional rather than unconditional love. If we lack the experience of being affirmed despite of our misdeeds, it becomes difficult to accept that God can forgive us. The punitive parent is often the model we internalise as a symbol of God's relationship with us. In contrast to this, redemptive love is an overwhelming gift. Christ alone could offer this to God on our behalf. One of the most powerful sentences in the Scriptures is Christ's petition: 'Father, forgive them; they do not know what they are doing.'[5] These words, spoken as Christ was nailed to the cross, continue to echo in the awareness of my need to forgive myself because he has forgiven me. In theory, I know that Christ's own sacrifice of his life is the redemptive reality of my belief in God and my relationship with him and all others. This is where true freedom lies. But to live in that realm requires me to be free from fear. Only then can I own my failures before God and those whom I have hurt. This is a daily challenge for me.

To acknowledge the need to forgive oneself as Christ forgives invites all of us to take risks. It does not mean that we adhere to a set of rules and regulations, but that we seek to live by the courage of our convictions. Cornelia Connelly, the foundress of my congregation, the Society of the Holy Child Jesus, was a pioneer whose following of Christ was unequivocal. I felt drawn to join this congregation because I could identify with Cornelia's challenge: 'Be yourself, but make that self who God wants it to be.' This is an ongoing process.

Joan Chittister addresses this similarly in her recent book *In the Heart of the Temple*. As a Benedictine sister, she is rooted in monasticism but, like Thomas Merton, extends her spiritual foundation to the needs of the whole world. I can resonate with that. It delights me that she also includes Jewish spirituality in her concept of an inclusive spirituality. She writes:

'In Jewish spirituality, for instance, two concepts dominate and are intertwined. The one *devekut*, translates as "clinging to God" or contemplation; the other *tikkun o'lam* translates as "repairing the world" or the works of justice. One without the other – contemplation without justice, clinging to mystery without repairing the real world – is unfinished, the tradition teaches, is dark without light, is grand without great, is soul without body.'[6] To depend totally on God's grace and to desire to repair the world demands that we start that process within ourselves.

At the beginning of this chapter, I posed the question: 'Where *is* God in this?' The thought that comes to me now is that God is asking me: 'Where are you, Eva, in this process of forgiving yourself?' The question is unsettling. It demands an answer. The fact is that, literally speaking, I cannot forgive myself. I do not have that power. I have denied my faith and relationship with Christ many times. But it is precisely through Christ's forgiveness of my repeated failures that I am glimpsing something of the power of his love. In the light of that realisation, I too can take steps to begin to forgive myself. Like a child who is starting to walk, I am likely to fall many times. But if I allow God's love to lift me up, I will eventually learn to walk by the power of that love.

My hope is that he will continually open our eyes and senses to see him in the events of our daily lives as we continue to journey with each other in faith, hope and love. In the light of his love, we can let go of the fear that we are unlovable. We need to be nourished in our spiritual roots from which we can draw strength to forgive and be forgiven and above all to forgive ourselves. The Jesuit Gerard Hughes expresses this idea in the following prayer:

'Come, Holy Spirit, and give my heart's dry roots your nurturing rain. Save me from the unbelief of lingering guilt, from harbouring grudges and nursing resentments. Open my eyes to the limitlessness of your goodness when, on the cross, you absorbed the violence of our sinfulness and gave us life in return. May your forgiving Spirit live in us now and always. We ask you this through Jesus Christ, our Lord. Amen.'[7]

It is the recognition of Christ's forgiving Spirit within me and all of us that enables me to say: 'I am learning to forgive myself.' In the spiritual life, there is no age limit to the learning process. Each day is a new beginning.

Memories of the past can be reached and brought back into the light without fear. When the soil is not ploughed, the rain cannot reach the seeds; when the leaves are not raked away, the sun cannot nurture the hidden plants. So also when our memories are covered with fear, anxiety or suspicion, the word of God cannot bear fruit.[8]

7

TREES DON'T TALK

Trees are sanctuaries.
Whoever knows how to listen to them,
can learn the truth.[1]

Hermann Hesse

IN THIS CHAPTER, I want to talk about 'talking to trees'. You might be wondering if I am a dotty old lady who believes that trees can talk to us in our language and that we can converse with them. Who could believe that? But I maintain that we *can* commune with trees. They provide us with the opportunity to still our inner storms. They communicate with us – through silence! So the plot thickens. Life is full of hidden mysteries. I am hoping that you'll take a risk and stay with me to unravel this one, which claims that talking with trees, listening to trees, sitting by trees, brings us closer to wisdom than we can imagine. I want to share with you three very different experiences, which have shown me how trees can play a significant part in our spiritual growth.

The first led me to realise that trees can offer us sanctuaries. When our thoughts are troubled, fearful or angry, a tree can provide us with a sense of reassurance that 'all will be well'. Their silent presence conveys a language of compassion and understanding. This can touch something deep within us. Trees have time to listen. They are never in a hurry to move on. Many of them are likely to outlive us. The life cycle of a tree has something to say to us about our own hopes that death is not the ultimate end but a passage into new life.

The second relates to the symbolism of a Tree of Life which I saw exhibited in the British Museum. It conveys a wordless message of peace. It came into being because the people of Mozambique handed in their weapons of mass destruction in exchange for tools that would be used to rebuild their land after years of bitter warfare.

The third image of trees reveals something of their healing power when our lives are torn and words cannot be found to express our feelings.

I often feel the need to remind myself of the claim that 'trees don't talk'. Their existence, in season and out of season, is their greatest gift to us. As long as I can remember, trees have been my companions and teachers throughout the changing seasons of my life. When I try to envisage a world without trees, something in the depth of my being becomes rigid, lifeless and fearful. Their presence offered me welcome and space to enter into my inner world where I struggled with the complexities of life. Adults tend to think that children have no real worries, but that is a myth. As a six-year-old there were many daunting shadows in my daily experiences. I sometimes wonder how it might have been had I been able to share these thoughts with my grandparents. Unfortunately I never knew them because they died before I was born. That has always been a sad loss for me. It was only through other children that I learnt how supportive they could be. According to my friends, grandparents were indeed 'grand'. They listened as trees do, without taking sides. They were people of great wisdom.

Even in my earliest years I was aware that I lived at two levels: the outer one was visible for everyone to see, but my inner life was a carefully guarded secret. It gave me a sense of great power. A particular contretemps with my father might illustrate this. I was probably about seven years old. I cannot remember the actual reason that caused him to reprimand me. But in true Victorian style his 'lectures' tended to go on endlessly and often ended with a punishment. On this occasion, when he had finished speaking, he asked: 'What have you got to say for yourself?' Apparently I answered: '*Ich denk mir mein Teil*.' It is difficult to translate this verbatim, but the meaning of my reply was: 'For my part, I keep my own thoughts to myself.' For once, my father was speechless! That was not the answer he had expected. He told me to go to my room, but he did not chastise me. From early childhood onwards I always had a sense that no one could reach into the depth of my being as I alone had the key to that inner place of my reality. It gave me a mysterious sense of power. I recall several occasions when I stood demurely before my father, whilst inwardly telling him what I thought about him, knowing that if he had even the remotest awareness of what was in my mind, the consequences would have been dire.

Many years later, when I was attending courses in child development, I became aware how authentic these experiences were. Now, seven decades on, I realise that such early self-awareness resulted in my becoming a very private individual. I was cautious with whom I chose to share my inner reality. Reflecting on this now, I find myself smiling at how such an incident in my early childhood has continued to empower me throughout my life. None of us can avoid being affected by injustice but if we can draw on our hidden strength of integrity, we are less likely to be overcome by tyrants we may meet in our lives.

Having said that, we still need someone with whom we can share our deepest thoughts. Most children have best friends with whom they can exchange secrets. But even as a young child I felt that it was inappropriate to talk about my home difficulties. This led me to the trees. Not only were they beautiful to look at, they were true listeners and real friends. I would sit quietly under a gnarled tree and unburden my heart. The extraordinary thing was that not only had I a sense of being heard, but that the silence of the tree provided a mutual respect and understanding between us. Whatever our age, it is always a great gift to know that someone has listened to what we are feeling, without passing judgement on us. My experience of being listened to often helped me to 'cool down' and perceive things from a different angle. The awareness of trees as patient and non-judgemental listeners doubtless contributed to that process.

But it is not only the visible trees which have played a significant part in my life journey and my awareness of the spiritual dimension of that process. There are also invisible trees which are still connected to us even though they disappeared from sight many thousand years ago.

I am reminded of my early recollections of many happy summers spent on the Baltic coast. I had been told there were sunken forests deep under the sea and that the resin of the trees formed amber. Like all children, I collected shells of every shape and size, hoping that I might also find some little pieces of golden nugget. My mother had beautiful necklaces and brooches made from these semi-precious stones.

Although I never had the joy of finding amber, I realise now that there is a connection between my spiritual journey and the sunken forests of pine trees. It lies with the resin which produced amber, long after the trees had been submerged. The demise of those trees and the eventual transformation of their resin – over a period of millions of years – highlights something of my faith journey and my belief in life after death. People of many different faiths believe in an afterlife. Even before I became a Christian I sensed that death was not the end of our existence, but a passage from one life to the next. I am awed by the symbolism of the image of amber. Having spent years in the depth of the ocean, it eventually rises from the sunken forests as a powerful sign of resurrection. These are phenomena which speak to my heart. At times they are more powerful than words. They nourish my faith.

In my family each of us chose different paths of faith and probably held contrasting views about life after death. Such diversity can appear to be divisive. There were certainly periods when I felt that my path was a lonely one. But, over the course of time, I have realised that the differences in our faith journeys were not necessarily discordant. We learnt to listen to one another and gradually found that this opened our hearts and minds to an understanding and acceptance of each one's uniqueness. Following a chosen path of faith can be costly, but experience tells me that this is worth every step. Wolfgang von Goethe, a German poet who lived in the eighteenth century, echoes my thoughts. He wrote:

'Our destiny sometimes has the appearance of a fruit tree in winter. Looking at its dreary aspect, who could think that the stiff branches, these jagged twigs, will turn green again and bloom next spring and then bear fruit? Yet this we hope, this we know.'[2]

As I look back to my first encounters with trees I realise that they encourage me to believe that our inner strength lies in our invisible roots. Trees survive icy winters, regain strength to flower in spring and bear fruit in summer. In this sense they continue to speak to me in the latter years of my life.

The language of trees is not through words as we use them, but through symbolism. I have met many people for whom trees have been life-giving symbols. A common example is the Tree of Life. It features in many cultures. When I heard that such a tree had been placed in the British Museum in London I could not imagine what this might be, though I knew that it was made out of disused weapons. Nothing could have prepared me for the impact of this sculpture when I eventually came face to face with it. The tree stands alone in the entrance hall. A brief description states: 'Made with decommissioned weapons from Mozambique's civil war, the Tree of Life sculpture is one of the centrepieces of Africa at the British Museum. Through the "Transforming Arms into Tools" programme, funded by Christian Aid, people in Mozambique handed in guns in exchange for sewing machines, bicycles, even tractors. The weapons were dismantled and the artists of the Nucleo de Arte made sculptures out of them.'

Reading the inscription I became aware that others too had been captivated by the tree. There was a meaningful silence, which I associate with churches, but not with museums. It was a profound experience realising that every part of that tree – even the birds, lizards, spiders and other creatures placed on the ground – had been made out of death-dealing weapons. Up to now, I had associated the tree of life with two powerful symbols. The first is from the book of Genesis in the Hebrew Scriptures, where we are given the idyllic picture of Adam and Eve in paradise and learn of their banishment when they had disobeyed God's command not to eat from the tree of life. The second tree is the cross of Christ, sometimes referred to as the Christ tree. It symbolises Christ's ultimate gesture of sacrificial love for the redemption of the world. These may not be easy concepts to integrate in our daily faith journeys. But as I stood by the Tree of Life created from scrapped weapons, I glimpsed something of Christ's redemptive love for us. Tears welled up within me and I walked out of the museum into the African garden, which had been created by the same group of artists as the Tree of Life. It was a sunny morning and the crowds had not yet arrived. As I wandered round from one sculpture to another I might indeed have been in the garden of Eden. The trees and bushes formed a fitting background for the carved creatures – great and small. It was not difficult to imagine the energy which flowed from the artists into those creations. But it was hard to absorb the fact that every piece of the armoury used to mould the sculptures had been part of a weapon, made to kill. The garden was small, but the design so powerful. There were also African plants and flowers proclaiming new life and beauty, as well as wooden carvings, speaking of hope for the future.

I have been to the museum and the garden several times, and on each occasion there has been a deepening of my awareness that this is not merely a beautiful and challenging exhibition, but a profoundly spiritual experience. The exhibition has now been moved, but the insights which this tree of life gave me will remain deeply imbedded in my consciousness for the rest of my life. This kind of experience convinces me that trees and other phenomena of nature can speak to us of eternal values.

You might like to pause at this point to wonder in what ways you too have been touched by a tree or some other natural phenomenon like a vivid sunset, a river or a flower. What aspect of the object holds your attention? Its beauty, its brokenness, its colour? It is good to be still for a while and allow ourselves to sink into the silence of our hearts.

I keep a picture of the tree next to my computer and never tire of spending some quiet moments with it. Like many true pieces of art this sculpture lends itself to individual interpretations. For me the tree is a symbol of Christ's cross. It is a resurrection tree, for its twigs bear new leaves. There are two main branches on either side of the trunk, but there are also smaller leaf-covered ones growing from the centre of the tree, upwards and outwards.

The transformation of weapons into such a work of

art gives me heart that I, too, can be transformed and the destructive elements within me can be recast into life-giving creations. This is not something that can happen all at once. The people of Mozambique must have struggled for a long time before putting their dreams of peace into reality.

I would like to think that this tree moves many hearts through the mystery of its silence. It is by its presence that it can reach out to all who are open to be touched, not by words but by deeds. The tree does not need to speak, as we do, but it presents messages we need to hear. It reminds me of the writings of the prophet Isaiah, 750 years before the birth of Christ:

'Peoples without number will ... say: "Come, let us go up to the mountain of Yahweh, to the Temple of the God of Jacob that he may teach us his ways so that we may walk in his paths;" ... He will ... adjudicate between many peoples; these will hammer their swords into ploughshares, their spears into sickles.'[3]

Weapons can indeed be turned into ploughshares, and in that process people who have been at war can become messengers of peace. The words of the prophet Isaiah and, in our present time, the process of reconciliation led by Nelson Mandela and Archbishop Tutu in South Africa, bear witness to this. Their ideals inspire me to lay down my own weapons of resentment and to start the long trek of reconciliation and peace.

The third example of the power of silence stems from the experiences of a young boy and the tree he chose to trust with his innermost feelings, which he was unable to put into words.

Clive was twelve when I first met him. He lived on a housing estate with his mother in the east end of

London. Racial tensions were fraught and Clive, who was Afro-Caribbean, was singled out to be bullied by a group of local boys. He was even sexually abused by them. So devastated was he by their attacks that Clive was frightened to leave his home, even when he was accompanied by his mother. Clive had been a bright, energetic student, but now refused to go to school because he feared he would meet some of the boys who had abused him. Eventually, he was offered a place at a boarding school financed by the Inner London Education Authority. It was there that I met him when I was employed as a psychiatric social worker. The school was outside London in a beautiful country area. I visited fortnightly, working with some of the emotionally disturbed boys. Clive was added to my list and came to see me regularly. He was always on time, but in the initial sessions chose not to speak. In his class he was one of the brightest pupils, but he was also a loner. He used his time with me to draw a variety of pictures, but declined to comment on them. Towards the end of the term, he drew a tree. It was a detailed drawing of a young sapling. I asked him if he could tell me something about it. He smiled, for the first time, but remained silent. When it was time for him to go, he picked up the drawing and gave it to me. I asked again if he could tell me something about the tree. He shook his head, but, as he was going towards the door, he said: 'I'll show it to you next week, if you like.' When he came the follow-ing time, it was he who initiated the conversation: 'Do you still want to see my tree?' I nodded and he led the way to a small spinney at the end of the playing fields where a number of young trees had been planted. One of them, a silver birch, stood slightly apart like an isolated child in a school playground. The wind was dancing with the young leaves and the sunshine drew patterns on the silvery trunk. Sadly some of the bark at the foot of the tree had been torn. 'This is my crying tree,' said Clive. In his anguish he had kicked the tree, hence the broken bark. We sat down on the grass and Clive leaned against the tree. There was a long silence. Then he said: 'I don't need to cry anymore, because I have a friend now.' He told me that the tree had become a friend he felt he could trust. Here he could pour out his fears and his anguish. The tree was always there with him and for him. It received his rage as well as his trust. The scars at the foot of the trunk bore witness to this process. We spent the rest of the session in silence under the leaves of the tree and the gentle sound of a soft breeze.

There was only one more session before the end of the term. Clive arrived punctually as usual and sat down to draw. After a while he said, 'Thanks for listening.' This might seem a surprising remark, given that most of our therapy sessions had been marked by silence. But therapy means healing. It comes from the Greek word, *therapeia*. Trees and therapists share this in common: it is often through silent communication that healing can take place. I thanked Clive for showing me his secret tree. At the end of the session he gave me the drawing he had been working on. It was a large green tree, filling the length and breadth of the page. 'It's for you,' he said, smiling as he left the room.

Fortunately I had a sensitive supervisor with whom I could share my experiences of the sessions with Clive. She too felt that the silence of our initial sessions were life giving for him. The tree had become his therapist and our meetings merely supported and validated the process.

The following term, Clive arrived on time again for his first session. More than a month had elapsed since our last meeting. He did not sit down to draw, but instead sat facing me. He told me that he now had a friend in his class. Clive had shown him his tree and they often went there together to talk or read. 'I think I'll be OK now,' he said. We agreed to go on meeting until half-term. At these sessions he talked most of the time, though occasionally chose to draw or paint. A tree always featured in his pictures.

There is no doubt in my mind that the young silver birch played a most significant part in Clive's recovery. Such an experience confirms for me the close connection we all have with the world of nature. When I look back on my early childhood I marvel that I grew up with such a deep awareness of the presence of trees. This laid the foundation of my later search for spiritual truths. I have valued that throughout my life.

Amber nuggets rising from the depth of the sea bed; a Tree of Life constructed from death-dealing weapons; an abused twelve-year-old boy healed by a silver birch: what can these three stories teach us? The first story, I think, reveals our need for silence. I do not mean a negative silence without sound, but the creative silence of the heart. It is within that serenity that seeds of faith can be nurtured. To be enfolded in such stillness is not an escape from reality, but a leap of faith which allows us to dare to hope in the power of God's redemptive love for all his creatures. It connects us with our need to be rooted in faith and strengthened by the light of the Holy Spirit from above. The small child searching for nuggets of amber knew nothing about faith journeys, but she drew on the life-force within her to begin the search.

The weapons of war transformed into a Tree of Life invite us to look at our deepest desires. They challenge us to choose between death and life for ourselves as well as others. The tree enables us to renew faith and hope in the depth of our being. There is no doubt that we live at a time when violence has escalated and the development of instruments of destruction threatens the existence of our planet. The Tree of Life is a symbolic reminder that peaceful solutions are available to resolve long-standing conflicts.

Clive's journey from the darkness of fear into the light of life was about transformation. When his trust in human beings had been shattered, his chosen tree helped him rebuild his inner brokenness. There comes a point in life when we need to give birth to ourselves. That can be a painful and risky business. Clive took that risk and chose life.

When we approach a tree
we approach a sacred being who can teach us about love
and endless giving.
She is one of millions of beings who provide our air,
our homes, our fuel, our books.
Working with the spirit of the tree can bring us renewed
energy, powerful inspiration, deep communion.[4]

8

TREE MOTHERS

*High on the mountains and in continuous
   danger,
the most indestructible, the strongest,
the ideal trees grow.*[1]

Hermann Hesse

EVERY TIME I read these words of Hesse, I
imagine three trees silhouetted on a distant
mountain top. Their roots are ancient. The trees
bring to mind three women who have accompanied me,
one way or another, in my ongoing journey in faith. But
they span 2000 years of time.

The central tree symbolises Mary, the mother of
Jesus. On either side are my own mother, Trude, and my
'spiritual' mother, Cornelia Connelly, the foundress of
my order, the Society of the Holy Child Jesus. Trude and
Cornelia were born in the nineteenth century, Mary
much earlier. So, I ask myself, what is it that these
women have in common? Like strong trees on mountain
tops they have experienced storms, which tore at their

roots, as well as warmth and sun which gave them strength to grow upwards towards the light. Their presence has a timeless message of hope.

Each of these women was married, experienced the joys and pains of childbirth, and the insecurities of uprooting and living as foreigners in strange surroundings. Their hopes and dreams, which all of us have when we are young, were shattered by unforeseen events. But Mary and Cornelia were sustained by their faith in God. Each had a sound spiritual grounding and the desire to fulfil God's will, whatever the cost. For my mother, it was slightly different. The traumas she had to face occurred before she had a conscious awareness of God. But 'grace builds on nature', as I was taught in the noviciate. Just as the roots of a tree grow in the dark, so does our awareness of God dawn in the depths of our being. There, small seeds can lie dormant for many years.

Mary, Cornelia and Trude all started life within the security of their own family circles. This was certainly true of my mother, who had a happy, carefree childhood. Her musical gifts were encouraged and she became a competent pianist. Cornelia also came from a secure background. She, too, was artistic and musically talented. I would imagine that Mary was brought up with songs and music integral to Jewish liturgy and life. In short, these women were nurtured by the traditions of their own families and wider communities. None of them could have had any inkling as to what would lie ahead.

Bearing in mind that we often meet God through the daily events of our lives, I want to reflect on significant episodes which shaped these three women. I hope they will also resonate with you and perhaps shed light on your own experiences which might have led to unexpected changes in your life. Such watersheds can be earth shattering, but they can often lead us into a deeper awareness of God's plans: 'I know the plans I have in mind for you ... plans for peace.'[2]

My first thoughts concern Mary's encounter with the angel, who announced that God had chosen her to be the mother of the Messiah. She was perplexed by this vision, since she was already engaged to Joseph. Neither of them would have expected anything so disruptive to their faith. Nor would it have been easy for Mary to confide in Joseph. For both, this was a challenge to trust that God would bring light into their inner darkness. When we are confronted with events which shatter our own plans, we are often challenged to trust God at a level we have not experienced previously. This is particularly true when we cannot explain to others why we deviate from the mores of our social/religious roots. Outwardly, it might seem that a spiritual encounter is unreal – a figment of the imagination – but inwardly its authenticity assures us that we have not fabricated it. We know that this is so because, in spite of our initial anxiety, we experience inner peace. This can empower us to respond to God's will even though it leads us where we might prefer not to go.

Mary's response to the angel: 'Let what you have said be done to me,' was also echoed later by Joseph who had a dream of an angel sent by God to warn him that Herod planned to slaughter all male babies. The angel instructed him: 'Get up, take the child and his mother with you, and escape into Egypt, and stay there until I tell you, because Herod intends to search for the child and do away with him.'[3] Joseph responded instantly. He led Mary and the infant Jesus to Egypt to avoid the massacre. The living out of our often frail faith can become a lifelong journey.

So how does Mary's experience resonate with the stories of my mother and Cornelia? My mother, too, was led to make drastic changes in her life. As a family, we also had to escape a tyrant who intended to slaughter Jews. My father had already made arrangements for my older brother, Dick, to finish his education in Switzerland. He was 17 when he left the family. I often wonder how my mother had the strength to part from him and later from my sister and me. She had no assurance that we would ever meet again. As I have already explained, my father had to leave her unexpectedly, as he had been warned that his arrest by the Nazis was imminent. Many years later my mother, sister and I reflected on these events. We had good reason to thank God for the survival of our family. Our spiritual journeys took different paths, but we were led by the same Spirit.

On the surface, Cornelia's faith journey may seem very different to the experiences of Mary and my mother. Cornelia's early life was sheltered and calm. She was happily married to an Episcopal priest. They settled first in Mississippi, USA, and then in Louisiana. They had five children. Cornelia had a deep faith in God, confirmed by her diary entries. She struggled with the awareness that her love of God was conditional. She prayed: 'If all this happiness is not for your greater honour and glory, take it from me.' In my early years in religious life, I found that sentence incomprehensible. Would a loving God deliberately bring sorrow into our lives? I could more easily identify with St Augustine's prayer of dedication to God, because Augustine added the words: 'But not yet!' Over and over again, I marvel at God's infinite patience with each one of us.

Often, when we least expect it, events can occur that change our lives radically. This happened to Cornelia. One day she was in the garden with her youngest child, John Henry, who was two-and-a-half years old. He was playing with the family's Newfoundland dog. They were running around and accidentally knocked against a vat of hot sugar cane. The burning liquid scalded John Henry. His mother held him for long agonising hours before he eventually died in her arms. During that painful time she struggled to accept that in a mysterious way God was present with her in this tragedy.

The date was 2 February 1840, the feast of the purification, when, in Jewish tradition, sacrificial offerings were brought to the temple in thanksgiving for the birth of a male child. In Christianity this is also an important feast, combining that ancient tradition with the recognition that the infant Christ himself was presented in the temple. Mary and Joseph brought two turtle doves as an offering of thanksgiving. It was the old priest Simeon's recognition that Mary's baby was the Messiah that led him to rejoice in this unexpected meeting. But Simeon also foretold the suffering that lay ahead for Mary and her son. St Luke tells us that 'his mother stored up all these things in her heart.'[4] This phrase also became meaningful for Cornelia in the many unexpected challenges she was called to face in the years ahead.

One of Cornelia's biographers, Sister Radegunde Flaxman SHCJ, gives us an insight into her spirituality when she comments on Cornelia's reflections written after the death of John Henry. The entry is brief, and made with deliberate care; words and format significant to the mother who made it:

'(John Henry) fell a victim on Friday – suffered 43 hours and was taken into the temple of the Lord on the Purification.'

Radegunde explains: 'Here is an epitaph, hidden away on a single page in a woman's small notebook. The outsider gazing at the page is led to the edge of some oblation where Cornelia seems to have been drawn into the sacrificial love of both the God incarnate and his mother. The depth of her desire to always remain in that attitude herself appears in her notebook on 9th February, a mere week later (i.e. after the tragic death of John Henry). Personal sorrow has not obliterated her readiness to offer herself unconditionally to God and she is sure this desire stems from him. She will contemplate Jesus in his suffering, she says, through the eyes of his mother and begs him to give her a share in Mary's steadfast compassion. This she did constantly until her death, turning to Our Lady of Sorrows at every crisis.'[5]

Only relatively recently – during the past twenty years – have I grown to appreciate fully both Mary and Cornelia. In earlier times, their attitude to suffering tested my limited comprehension. Now I feel I am beginning to catch glimpses of the depth of their love for Christ in response to his love for them. I can understand the meaning of compassion and Cornelia's desire to share with passionate love the sacrificial offering of Christ on the cross. This also deepens my understanding of the vows I made 45 years ago. I remember an elderly sister in our congregation, saying: 'When you make your vows, offering the whole of your life to God, it is like signing a blank cheque of all your life and giving it to him.' It is often in the face of cruel events that I am reminded of that truth. But God is never outdone in love. We may not recognise this when tragedy strikes us, but my own experience along with what I have learnt from my mother shows me that in the midst of fear and disbelief God is present in our life. His love sustains us in the darkest times.

This was certainly my mother's experience during the last weeks she spent alone in Germany to oversee the packing up of the furniture and all our belongings. During the day, she was relatively safe in the house, but not during the night. There was a real possibility that she could be arrested, once it was dark. That was the usual procedure when a group of 'storm troopers', the Nazi's secret police, would knock in the pitch black. But my mother was sheltered by members of the underground movement whose courage and bravery were seldom recognised. By protecting her, they endangered their own lives as well as those of their families. Each evening, mother would leave our house after dark to find shelter at different safe addresses she had been given. She would return at dawn, in time to open the door to the team of men who were packing all our furniture and belongings, prior to sending them to a warehouse. Many years later, when she was able to talk about these events with my sister and me, it became clear that mother was sustained and protected by the love of God even before she was able to recognise it as from him.

Mary, Cornelia and my mother learned the meaning of sacrificial love through their life experiences. God, who so often seems to be distant, revealed himself not only in the events but through people who willingly shared in each other's suffering. Such examples of superhuman love cannot be fabricated by our own efforts.

When I visualise the trees of Hermann Hesse I am made aware that their strength lies in their roots. Similarly, our rootedness in faith enables us to withstand the often unexpected storms of our lives. But precisely because roots are channels of life, they not only preserve us in our brushes with death, but also strengthen us to celebrate life here and now, even amidst the darkness that can descend suddenly and envelop us.

This is especially so, when I think of my mother and recall her warmth, vitality, humour and *joie de vivre*. In spite of all she endured, these qualities were never obscured. She was above all a generous person who experienced many losses in her life as well as deep grief, but she never lost hope. If she could have seen the trees Hesse described, she would have admired their fortitude and resilience. Not for a moment would she have identified herself with their dignity and beauty. But these characteristics are ones which I often recall. Even when she was uprooted and very short of money, she retained her inner dignity. Her spirit was undaunted.

I have never forgotten one particular occasion when my mother's generosity touched my heart. During my first year at boarding school, she visited me on my thirteenth birthday. She carried a carefully wrapped present. When I took it from her, it felt as though it might be books. I was an ardent reader. As I unwrapped the parcel, I felt a softness. She had brought me two leather-covered books of Mozart and Beethoven piano sonatas – one red and the other green. Even at that age, I was deeply moved because I realised that although we were now refugees my mother had managed to save money from her meagre salary as a cook, to buy something which connected with our family roots. She had spotted these editions in a secondhand bookshop and hoped they would still be available for her when she had saved sufficient money to pay for them. I have never forgotten the pride with which she presented them to me. Playing the sonatas always reminded me of her love and the secret sacrifices she had to make in her life.

I have often heard it said that a sense of humour is a saving grace. It was certainly so for my mother on many occasions during her struggles to learn English. She had the gift of being able to laugh at herself as well as laugh with others – but never at others. Cornelia, too, had that ability, but I think she may have been less spontaneous than my mother. It would be hard to imagine that Mary, a Jewish woman, was without humour. The Jewish tradition has a fund of humour, deeply embedded in its culture. But, alas, the image we have inherited of Mary does not reveal her laughing, playing or being relaxed. The nearest example I have found of this is a small black carving of Mary with Jesus as a toddler. It was crafted in Nigeria. Mother and son are playing together and there is real joy and laughter in this image. I also know of another vibrant carving displayed on the front cover of Tina Beattie's book *Rediscovering Mary*. It depicts a bronze sculpture by Maureen Coatmen, at the church of St Luke, Duston, Northamptonshire. This shows Mary dancing with her young son, with a hint of a smile on

Mary's face. Her hair is blown by the wind and the child is leaping towards her. There is a sense of joyful abandonment. I can almost hear them singing and laughing together.

As I reflect on the individual faith journeys of my mother, Cornelia and Mary, I am struck by the paradox of the uniqueness of each person and the universality of suffering which leads to new life. Central to this is Christ's crucifixion and resurrection. Tina Beattie expresses this with her insight as a mother as well as a feminist theologian. She writes:

'Throughout the ages, Mary ... remains a constant motif in the faith of those who suffer and who find in her capacity for suffering a source of solidarity and solace. Mary on Calvary is both mother and companion of all who find themselves in that place where no one chooses to stand. She is at the heart of grief and loss and betrayal, but that darkest moment in history is also the greatest moment of love and faith.'[6]

Mary, Cornelia and my mother encountered many life-giving and death-dealing experiences. When we become aware of the uniqueness of this process in our own lives we, like Mary, grow in understanding of the mystery of God's love for each of us. Cornelia experienced this many times. For instance, when her marriage broke up and later, when she was asked by Pope Gregory XVI to found a new religious order for women in England. In her acceptance of every new challenge in her life, her desire to give herself totally to God was strengthened. It might not immediately appear that a loving God could be pivotal to such events. On the contrary, the events themselves might be felt as a series of death blows. It is within this darkness, however, that new light can shine. Spiritual birth and death are mysteriously intertwined. Nowhere is this more clearly shown than on Calvary.

When I envisage the group who stood at the foot of the cross of Jesus, I feel my own fear and coldness. I too want to run away like the disciples, but am held by the bond of love of those who are there to support Mary and her son. I had the privilege to be present many times during my work with people with HIV/AIDS, when a loved partner, son or daughter was dying. Repeatedly, those of us who were there felt empowered by the person whose life was ebbing away. At such moments love becomes almost tangible. Even in the experience of the brutal agony of Christ's crucifixion, it seems that Mary and her companions were drawn into the mystery of Christ's sacrificial love. It was Jesus himself, who pointed to a new birth in the life of this small gathering when he said to Mary: 'Woman, this is your son.' And to John: 'This is your mother.'[7]

At the time of her son's final agony, Mary was called to be mother of the infant church. It is often through death that new life emerges.

As I have not experienced motherhood, I may never be able to understand fully the sorrows of Mary and Cornelia over the death of a son. But I have learnt something from my mother's anguish at the time of the death of my brother. Dick was the eldest child in our family. He and I had a close, invisible bond, though we never lived together after I was eleven. Dick's life was fraught from babyhood. He found the arrival of my sister difficult, exacerbated by the fact that it was clear as she grew older that she was particularly gifted intellectually. His gifts and mine lay elsewhere. My father always hoped that his son would achieve academic heights and this caused constant friction between them. Yet, when my parents' marriage broke up, Dick accompanied my father to America. For my mother this must have felt like a living death because there was no reassurance that she would ever see her son again. Father severed all ties with us and forbade my brother to communicate with us. My mother seldom talked about her grief. Fourteen years later, however, Dick contacted us to let us know that father had died.

Tentatively, letters were exchanged. It was a moving moment when Mother and Dick spoke with each other by phone. Subsequently, holiday visits followed and it was a great joy for mother, then in her seventies, to be reunited with her son. But this was a relatively short respite as Dick became ill and was diagnosed to be suffering from cancer. He asked if he could come 'home' to my mother and sister. Both were glad to have him but, in practice, it proved to be a very painful time for mother and son. There was too much unfinished business and too little time to be fully reconciled. Although she longed to be able to 'mother' him, she found it difficult to do so without 'smothering'. As Dick's illness progressed, their relationship became more fraught. However, on his last night, he sat up in bed and looked intently at each of us, saying: 'Thank you so very much.' Those were his last words and we treasured them. They planted the seeds of peace and reconciliation in our hearts. In time, they became a fruitful gift for each of us.

I stayed with Dick through the night. It was a serene time of watching and waiting. In the early hours of the morning, sensing he was gently drifting away, I called my mother and sister, just before he died peacefully. The fact that the three of us were able to share that sacred moment was a great gift.

Dick's death was a blessed relief because his suffering was ended, but inevitably mother's grief was ongoing. She wished that she could have done more for him before and during his illness. But, in time, she realised that Dick's coming home to be with her was ultimately a healing for both of them.

The image of Hermann Hesse's trees remains with me. Silhouetted on a mountain top they mirror something of the agony of Calvary. At times of profound anguish, we need such symbols, especially when we cannot verbalise our grief. In their simplicity, trees speak not in words but by their very existence. In the changing of the seasons they convey to us that the death of winter is followed by spring when new life emerges. Death does not have the final word.

Mary, Cornelia and Trude experienced this, each in their own uniqueness. Their lives reveal the power of God's redemptive love. I mentioned earlier that I see in the three trees a likeness to the crosses on Calvary. In times of grief and mourning, they draw me back to Christ's death and resurrection. Like the three trees, so my 'tree mothers' leave an enduring mark on my life. Each of them can be named as a 'beloved' by God. This is a challenge for me and perhaps also for all of us. Dare we open ourselves unconditionally to God as Mary, Cornelia and Trude did? By our own efforts this would be impossible, but with God all things are possible.

A tree uses what comes its way to nourish itself. By sinking its roots deeply into the earth, by accepting the rain which flows towards it, by reaching out to the sun, the tree perfects its character and becomes great ... That is the secret of the tree.[8]

9

ROOTS AND ECHOES

A tree says:
I live out the secret of my seed to the very end
I trust that God is in me.
Out of this trust I live.[1]

Hermann Hesse

AM WRITING on a hot day in May. It is a wake-up moment as the weather has changed at last. It has been unusually cold and capricious. I have been waiting to plant some seedlings, which will bring colour and joy into an otherwise grey and barren cul-de-sac. When I first came to live in central London I experienced it as a concrete jungle, but the area immediately outside the community's house has been transformed gradually by a variety of pot plants and window boxes. They provide a welcome to visitors as well as those of us who live here. Many of the plants arrive as 'plugs', carefully packed in small boxes. They usually come with a printed label asking: 'When we arrive, please allow us to rest for a day, as we have had a long journey. Then plant us gently and leave us in a warm place.' When the tiny roots begin to grow – initially like fine threads of cotton – they are transferred to seed trays filled with nourishing compost. There they continue to be cared for and are eventually taken outside to accustom themselves to the wider world. Once they are ready to go into tubs and window boxes, they are given a boost of special plant food, bedded down in their new home and watered regularly. As far as possible they are protected from predators.

This strikes me as an apt illustration of our connectedness with the whole of nature in its various guises. At a time when many people are rightly concerned about the destruction of the ozone layer through the misuse of our natural resources, a few window boxes are unlikely to make a significant difference to the greening of the universe. But they are a constant reminder that we have come into this world to preserve life and be co-creators with God, the source of that existence.

There is another aspect of these frail plants which gives me food for thought. When I see the first signs of rooting, I never cease to be surprised by the hidden strength in their thrust for life and their eagerness to fulfil their destiny. Their birth process makes me recall how we, too, started our earthly life from the fusion of two microscopic seeds. When we take time to reflect on this, we enter into the mystery of the wonder of our being.

The vulnerability of the plug plants also evokes other thoughts. The first strand of life, which forms the roots of each plant, heralds a sign of hope. It declares: 'I am alive! I am called into being and I will become what I am destined to be.' This has echoes in our human hearts. We too have a deep-rooted longing to fulfil our destiny. We cannot do so without the ongoing awareness that we are contingent beings in need of mutual support so that each of us can discover the gift of our uniqueness. John O'Donohue points to this when he writes:

'Like fields, mountains and animals we know we belong here on earth. However, unlike them, the quality and passion of our longing make us restlessly aware that we cannot belong *to* the earth ... '[2]

John O'Donohue opens my mind and heart to the fact that my earthly life is not my final destination, yet it is the transitory place where I can discover my true self in relationship with God, with others and myself.

There have been moments in my life when I longed to be rooted, but the older I have grown, the more I have come to realise that our existence here is transitory. If we try to put our roots down too firmly, we may well become 'stuck' and never arrive at our final destination. I am not suggesting that we should always be on the move, but that we look on life as an ongoing journey. One of the blessings of growth in maturity is the opportunity to reflect on our past with the light of experience and discover that we have not been travelling alone. It is a moment of relief and joy when it dawns that God's Spirit is deep within our being. It is here that we experience our true self in relationship with God.

This was brought home to me unexpectedly in the 1970s, when I was struggling with feelings of despair. My world seemed to be falling apart. I had lost my sense of direction and felt isolated. The faith which had held me rooted seemed to have shrivelled and the future looked menacing. Professed as a religious sister for ten years, I was now encountering many personal difficulties. I had reached a point when I began to feel I could no longer meet the challenges of living in a religious community. Fear of failure has often darkened my life and at that stage it seemed that God had abandoned me. I was grappling with this dilemma during a retreat in Ireland. Walking along a mountain path with woodland on one side and an arresting view of green valleys on the other, I felt drawn to leave the path and go deeper into the pine wood. I experienced a profound stillness there and, compared with the sunny path I had left, the wood seemed dark. A tree with gnarled roots caught my attention. It seemed to offer a comfortable resting place, so I sat there, in the hollow space between its roots, leaning back against the ancient trunk. An hour passed before I realised that the interplay of sunlight and darkness was touching something deep within me. I felt enfolded in the silence all around me as I watched the beams of light, dancing in and out of the trees. The paths leading further into the wood were also flecked by the changing light. At one point, I was drawn to a young tree transformed by the sun's rays. It appeared to me as a symbol of Christ's presence. I was reminded that he too experienced many challenging stages in his life on earth. Even when the sun moved, the tree remained a sign of hope as my own inner darkness was transformed by its light. The image is still rooted deep within me. When I eventually left the wood and resumed my walk along the path, I realised that the depression which had held me captive had shifted. I sensed that God's light had touched me in the darkness of the wood and watered my shrivelled roots. My faith began to grow again.

I have often reflected on this experience and value it as an important insight into the meaning of rootedness. We sometimes talk about our need to be rooted in love so that we might grow. The interplay of darkness and light in the wood reminded me that God is present, even when I am trapped in my own inner turmoil. He knows my love of trees and many times makes this his meeting place with me. The sense of my encounter with God enabled me to rediscover my faith in him. His light was more powerful than my darkness. We depend on him to water our roots, just as the small plug plants are reliant on us to care for them. In the light of that experience I can echo Hermann Hesse's words: 'I trust that God is in me.' Such echoes are life giving. They can reconnect us with our roots at times of tumult as well as in moments of stillness.

I remember an occasion when that happened during a holiday in Wales. I was sitting by a stream close to a waterfall, listening to the sounds around me. Magpies were chattering, swallows were dipping in and out of the water, a tree creeper was busy finding insects for her lunch. Somewhere, out of sight, a couple of sparrows were arguing while the wind rustled in the branches of a beech tree. The thought that struck me then was the diversity of life all around me and the richness of that experience. Later that evening, when I recalled that scene, another thought surfaced, like an echo which linked me to my own roots. I became aware of the multiplicity of gifts in my life, especially my Jewish ancestry and my adoption into the Catholic faith community. It was not the first time that I experienced such root-echoes. In the past I tended to deny my German-Jewish heritage. It made me feel isolated from my peer group. On this occasion, I could both own and welcome my past connections. The remembrance of Jewish musicians, poets and writers made me aware of the richness of my origins. I began to see them as gifts from God who creates in diversity, not in uniformity.

For countless generations, trees have been a source of wonder and wisdom. Thomas Merton felt this when he was a novice at a Cistercian monastery in Kentucky. He wrote:

'And now in the woods, I once again revisit the idea of simply staying here, in the woods – with great interior freedom, applying myself to the main business, which has nothing to do with places and does not require a beach of pure, white Caribbean sand. Only a silence and the curtain of trees.'[3]

As a young monk, Merton was touched by the power of trees and their connectedness with us. He, too, discovered that, throughout the changing of the seasons, they convey a solidity and rootedness which can be profoundly meaningful.

I experienced this myself in 1936, when my father planted young fruit trees in our garden in Freiburg. The cherry trees were my favourites. Watching the first blossoms emerge after the snow had melted filled me with delight. This was not only because I longed for the juicy Black Forest cherries, but also because there was something entrancing about these frail blossoms. They lasted for only a short time, but they conveyed a message which has remained with me for more than seventy years. Every season has a meaning and a beauty of its own. I was only in Freiburg for three springtimes but when I reflected on these many years later, I realised that the young trees offered me seeds of wisdom. The hope of fruitfulness and new life was evident in their fragile beauty. Their roots were embedded in the depth of the earth. Although I was afraid of darkness, I began to understand that there is another perspective to this: it is through darkness that growth takes place. That symbolism has frequently been an encouragement at difficult times in my life. Remembering the roots of our cherry trees makes me aware that we too need inner darkness as well as light. It is often through the experiences of such darkness that we find strength to grow and make significant changes in our lives.

Our garden was stony and the tender roots of the trees needed fertile soil. My father used to insist that we collect buckets full of stones to ensure that the young roots would not be crushed. It was not my favourite occupation; it felt more like a sentence of 'hard labour', but, in retrospect, I am glad that I could remove some obstacles to give root space to enable trees and other plants to grow. As I write this I smile, as I realise that it is they who have helped me to grow!

When I left Freiburg, I found it difficult to relinquish the house and garden. It was a painful uprooting, though I also wanted to move into safer surroundings. I thought I was leaving for ever, so I spent my pocket money on an illustrated book of the Black Forest. All the photos were in black and white – colour photography would come only later. But I still have that book and I treasure it. I bought it because it had so many meaningful memories of places, people and trees in and around Freiburg. During my early years in England, I found solace in leafing through this book and reliving the beauty of our home and our surroundings. I had no idea then that I would one day be able to return to Freiburg, revisit our house and pluck cherries from our trees. God is bountiful. He not only led me back to the house I loved, but has graced me with deep and meaningful relationships with the family who live there. Three generations have since grown up there. The fruitfulness of such friendships is priceless.

In the 1970s, when I was employed as a psychiatric social worker in a child guidance clinic in the east end of London, we worked with broken and dysfunctional families to enable them to restructure their lives. Each family needed different responses. With some, we encouraged them to plant seeds or bulbs, depending on the season. Simply caring for plants and helping them to grow can be the first steps to recovering our power to love and care for others who are more vulnerable than us. The children found this especially meaningful. They were proud that they could bring to life something as fragile as seeds. It was not difficult for them to make the analogy between the seeds and themselves. Caring for the seeds, nurturing and protecting them and sharing the delight of seeing them grow, had meaning not only for the children but also for their parents. One child said: 'I always water my mustard and cress seeds before I have breakfast.' It was easy for her to make the therapeutic connection of this very simple action. She discovered that there was good within herself and that she had the power to share that with others – not only with seeds. Her parents, too, learned that metaphorical watering of each other and their children produced growth in their relationships with one another.

Hesse's words: 'Out of this trust, I live' have also

given me food for thought. I wish that I could resonate with this phrase. I have always found it difficult to trust God, other people and myself. I used to wonder, in my younger days, if I would have found it easier to trust, had I been a 'cradle Catholic'. But I know now that God in his wisdom waited for a time when I could reflect on my life and discover the God who knew me and loved me long before I took the first wavering steps towards faith. Even now, I can identify with the story in the Bible of a father who begged Jesus to heal his son, who had severe epileptic fits from birth onwards. The father had asked Jesus' disciples to heal the boy, but they had been unable to do so. Imploring Jesus, the father cried out: 'If you can do anything, have pity on us and help us.'[4] I, too, have often turned to God as a last resort, urging him to calm my inner storms and frenzies. Christ's reply to the anguished father is challenging: 'If you can? Everything is possible for anyone who has faith.' The father's instant response came from the depth of his love for his son: 'I do have faith. Help the little faith I have!'[5] This is a prayer I often make my own.

My lack of unconditional faith confronts me time and again with the ongoing struggle to trust God implicitly. This is not only a problem for me, but for many people. Unlike trees, we have the power to make choices every day of our lives. But we are complex creatures and cannot always be sure of the sincerity and purity of our intentions. Our motives can often be clouded and mixed. We long to be free from our inner struggles, but we find it difficult to echo Christ's words in the garden of Gethsemane, where he prayed before his arrest and crucifixion: 'If it is possible, let this cup pass me by. Nevertheless, let it be as you, not I, would have it' and after further prayer, he said: 'If this cup cannot pass by without my drinking it, your will be done!'[6] There Christ experienced the extremities of his own inner struggle to accept God's will unconditionally. Faced with the horror of crucifixion, Christ also struggled to trust unconditionally. For me, this is one of the most poignant scenes in the gospels, for it highlights the vulnerable humanity of the Son of God.

Our hesitation to trust God when there is no logical explanation for the suffering which we or others endure is, I think, linked to our caution in loving unconditionally. Humanly speaking it is impossible to trust without reserve. Even Christ had to experience this before his arrest and crucifixion. But the purity of his love for his Father and the desire to be totally in accord with his will enabled him to offer himself unreservedly on our behalf.

Occasionally there are men and women who, like Maximilian Kolbe, a Catholic priest, can offer totally unconditional love. Father Kolbe had been sent to Auschwitz, one of Hitler's most notorious concentration camps. There, he offered his life in exchange for that of a married man who, along with other prisoners, was condemned to die of starvation. This brutal punishment was an act of revenge because a prisoner had escaped. Maximilian's offer was accepted by the guards and he became the last to die amidst the group of men chained and incarcerated in a dark cellar.

To trust God and to trust others is relatively easy when we compare it to the challenges we encounter in trying to trust ourselves. We live in a competitive world where we often experience others as more competent and able than we are. A surprising number of my friends and acquaintances have grown up with the notion that 'I am not as good as X'. This was certainly so in my own case as my parents tended to impress on me that my sister was a model of perfection which I should imitate. She was in every way 'the good girl' and I, in turn felt like 'the bad girl'. Her school reports were glowing; mine repeatedly reminded me 'Eva could do better'. Only in comparatively recent times have my sister and I been able to redress that inequality. But it has been a freeing experience for both of us. Our relationship as sisters has grown into an adult friendship, which is mutually supportive. This is a priceless gift. It has taken a long time for me to be able to believe in myself and recognise God's love and trust in me. It is out of that realisation that I have begun to grow in the certainty that it is possible for me to be 'love-able'. When we know we are loveable because God has planted the seeds of his love in the depth of our being, then we can take a leap into freedom. The shadows of the past no longer hold us captive.

I have reflected here on different aspects of Hesse's quotation, printed at the beginning of this chapter. But they are connected. It is only when I can accept that God's Spirit is in me, that I can relate freely with others. The sense of loneliness, which is often present within each of us, is not necessarily a negative reaction. It can be a positive reminder that God is waiting in the depth of our being. When we can find ways of responding to that awareness, the pain diminishes and can be transformed. Like Christ, we too need to create time and space to recharge our spiritual batteries. That is easier said than done, given the busy lives most of us lead. But if we really want this, we can find ways and means to create a space where our spiritual roots can be revitalised and where we can listen to echoes that come from our hearts.

Memories of the past can be reached and brought back into the light without fear. When the soil is not ploughed, the rain cannot reach the seeds; when the leaves are not raked away, the sun cannot nurture the hidden plants. So also when our memories are covered with fear, anxiety or suspicion, the word of God cannot bear fruit.[7]

10

THE WISDOM
OF TREES

Trees have long thoughts,
Long breathing thoughts,
Just as they have longer lives than ours.
They are wiser than we are.[1]

Hermann Hesse

HERE IS SOMETHING challenging about Hesse's words. They make me wonder: 'What is the meaning of wisdom? How and where do we find and experience wisdom in our ordinary everyday lives?' I am hoping that we might explore this together in this chapter.

In my childhood years, I revered trees as special companions. Now I recognise signs of a deeper mystery inherent in our connectedness with the whole of creation. This thought came to me recently when I read a passage from Satish Kumar's book *You Are, Therefore I Am.*[2] Satish was born and brought up in India. He was a Jain monk. His father died when he was young. Reflecting on his childhood, Satish writes:

'"Nature is the greatest teacher," said my mother while we were walking from home to our farm. "Greater than the Buddha," she continued, "for even he learned from nature. He became enlightened while sitting under a tree, contemplating on the compassionate, generous, evergreen tree. While observing the Banja tree under which he was sitting, the Buddha realised that the fulfilment and self-realisation of the tree was in its being that which it is, and never trying to be anything other than a tree. As tree it was always available to those who came to it: the birds could nest in it, the animals could rest under its cool shade and everyone could benefit from its fruit."'

Satish Kumar commented: 'I was only eight years old listening to my mother and yet it was something I could understand. She would talk to me in more or less the same way as she would talk to my older sisters and brothers. To her I was not a child – an undeveloped adult. She always talked to us of matters of great substance.'

The wisdom of this woman touches me deeply, particularly as I learnt that she was illiterate and had to use her thumb print to sign important documents. There is no doubt that she opened her children's hearts and minds to the wonders of nature and to the mystery of the creator spirit. A mother's word of wisdom may be a seed which flourishes and grows as trees do. Such seeds will bear fruit for many generations.

There is a longing within us to search for wisdom, to be guided by it and ultimately to love it. That is the treasure we hope to find in our pilgrimage here on earth. It may lead us into unknown territories. Will we be given signs and directions?

I have chosen Jane Gifford to point us in the ways of ancient wisdom which our forefathers and mothers valued. In her book *The Celtic Wisdom of Trees* she writes:

'Two thousand years ago, before the Roman invasion, Great Britain was largely a land of trees. Each species had its own particular treasure to offer in terms of shelter, energy, food and medicine.

'The Celts had a vast storehouse of knowledge about human relationship with the natural world. Specially trained elders, both men and women, committed the history and knowledge of their tribe to memory and passed it down in verse form through generations.'[3]

What strikes me about these words is that our early ancestors recognised how significant it was for us to be in harmonious relationship with the whole of nature. Trees were an important part of that scenario. They were revered for their age. Wisdom was attributed to them and likewise to elders in human families. In our consumer society we are in danger of losing the store of wisdom which past generations have handed down to us. But there are occasional signs which can give us hope that all is not lost.

I would like to share with you some moments in my life which have shed light on my understanding of the gift of wisdom. I hope these might also lead you down your own memory lanes to discover where wisdom has been at work within you.

Let me tell you an experience my mother had when she was in Austria for her yearly winter holiday with my sister. Mother was well into her seventies and, the previous year, her skiing instructor had persuaded her to retire. He felt that he could no longer take the responsibility of having someone of her age zigzagging down the mountain slopes. After fourteen years with the same instructor, this was a sad moment for mother but, none the less, she continued to return for several years, walking daily in the winter landscape. She loved seeing the sun sparkling on snow-covered pine trees. They were different from the other trees which were stripped of their leaves during the winter and had to wait patiently to be re-clothed in spring time. This made her think. Most of the trees were older than her, but were transformed into beautiful images in the winter season. They conveyed something about the hope of transformation in her life and other people's too.

One morning, as she returned from a stroll, she saw a girl coming towards her. The child was about five years old. As they met, they stood and looked at each other. The girl said to mother: 'Are you old?' Mother thought for a moment. Smiling, she replied: 'I don't know.' The child looked up earnestly and pronounced: 'You're not old. You have teeth. My granny is old. She doesn't have teeth.'

I love that story because it touches on the wisdom of children and the elderly. If one takes the encounter at surface level, it could simply be an amusing tale. But there might also be a deeper meaning to it. Each stopped to gaze at the other. Neither of them was in a hurry. This is unusual because we tend to be swept along by the tides and storms that often pressurise our daily lives. But for the child and my mother there was no need to be in a rush. When youth and age meet they often have something to offer each other. Elders are proverbially wise. They can often echo the wisdom of trees. They discern and draw on their own root experiences to grow in wisdom as well as age. But children, too, can be gifted with wisdom. In their simplicity, they may appear older than their years. The child offered my mother a word of encouragement. Mother knew that chronologically she was old but found this hard to accept. She missed her skiing classes! But following her conversation with the child, she could walk with her head high. There, in the silent beauty of the glistening landscape, wisdom touched both young and old. They could gaze at each other in silence and experience the invisible wisdom which touched their hearts.

This vignette may indicate the way wisdom often operates. In retrospect, we may discover that wisdom has been a hidden companion when we have had to grapple with painful or confusing events in our lives. When my mother was struggling to accept the inevitable diminishments of ageing, she toiled with the feelings of loneliness which touch us as we get older and realise we can no longer do some of the things we used to enjoy. At such times wisdom often accompanies us silently as we try to find our way through the dark woods of many different life experiences. Wisdom does not take away our pain of loneliness, but neither does it desert us. It waits patiently until we are sufficiently still to be able to receive gifts of new insights. When we have made that discovery, our hearts may lead us to a deeper search for wisdom.

Perhaps you too can recall an encounter with a wise person and how that individual supported you at a difficult stage of your life journey. The 'wisdom' person might have been a relative, a colleague, a friend or a stranger. It would be worthwhile to rest for a while and wander down memory lane to relive such an experience. These moments can reveal a deeper understanding of past events and strengthen us in our ongoing journey.

My own thoughts take me back to the ending of my noviciate in the Society of the Holy Child Jesus. I was due to make vows of chastity, poverty and obedience, in order to commit myself to God as a member of this congregation. I had been in the noviciate for three years preparing for this solemn moment. They were years of ups and downs but, during the final months, I really felt I had been called to give myself to God in this way. The Society had accepted me to become a member. Outwardly all the necessary steps had been taken and the ceremony was intended to confirm this through joyful celebration.

No one could have been more surprised than I was when fear gripped me the night before this solemn event. I felt that I could not possibly commit myself to God as a religious sister. Therefore I could not make my vows. The sense of terror overwhelmed me. I asked to see the Superior, Sister Teresa, one of the most outstanding women I have ever met. She was a deeply spiritual person and a sensitive counsellor and guide – though as far as I know she never had professional training in these skills. Rooted in her faith and love of God, Sister Teresa had a realistic understanding of the vagaries of human nature. Above all, she was a wonderful listener. I trusted her more than any other person I have known. Nothing could shock her.

We talked through the hours of the night and into the early morning. I found myself unlocking doors of my unconscious fears and anxieties. The quality of her listening enabled me to trust her. It was my first experience of speaking with someone who understood me better than I understood myself. She never underplayed the negative feelings I had about myself, but led me to the awareness of God's infinite love. As the new day dawned, I knew that the darkness within me had been transformed. We had a few hours' rest before the ceremony of vows which led me to a new stage in my ongoing spiritual journey. The year was 1960 yet it seems like only yesterday.

Reflecting on this experience, I am aware that the wisdom of God often touches us through others. Long before I was old enough to verbalise this, I was conscious of it deep within my being. I learnt it through my love of trees, and the time they gave me to absorb their wordless wisdom. Slowly, but surely, my roots grew into the faith which I could ultimately give expression to on that memorable night.

It is sometimes said that life is a journey into the unknown. Many of the choices we have to make are pragmatic and relatively easy. However, at a spiritual level, it becomes more complex. Just as our physical well-being requires an appropriate diet, exercise and rest, so our spiritual self has to be nourished too. For thousands of years, people have done this through prayer, meditation and reading. When I look at the current pattern of my prayer life I find myself struggling to balance my spiritual needs with all the active demands on my time. It is never easy to create a still place within oneself. Ideally I try to find moments when I can be assured of silence, but in our busy lives that is not always possible. I am often surrounded by external noises and also invaded by the restlessness inside me. I feel closest to God when I pray in woods or fields – away from the phone, my computer and other distractions. Living in central London, with all the noise and bustle of city life, makes it more difficult to create regular times of stillness and inner peace. It is, I think, a common experience for many of us, that the demands of action often eat into the time needed for prayerful contemplation. When this becomes a daily tension over many weeks and months, our prayer life can become dry and barren like a desert.

A short while ago I had an unexpected experience which has affirmed my belief that the Spirit of God can touch us at many unexpected moments in our pilgrimage. When this happens, our spiritual and physical energies can be revitalised.

The choir I sing in was giving an evening concert in central London. Our dressing room was crowded. The noise sounded like starlings chattering on the branches of a tree, each trying to get a balancing space for themselves. Within the turmoil I noticed that one woman was sitting crosslegged on the floor, with her back against a wall, totally absorbed in meditation. I could hardly believe what I was witnessing. Even though she was so unobtrusive, her presence radiated a tangible peace. Her eyes were closed and she seemed unaware of the flurry around her. We had an opportunity to talk during the interval and to share something of our faith journeys. We discovered that both of us began our lives from a non-Christian upbringing. She came from an Indian background and I from a nominally Jewish childhood. For each of us, prayer was now an important factor in our daily lives. I have often tried to pray on buses, trains and the underground, but I have never reached the depth of stillness so evidently achieved by this woman absorbed in meditation.

As I reflect on this gift – for this is how I perceived our encounter – it seems to me that we are like two different trees nourished by the Spirit of God. This person has inspired me to revitalise my spiritual roots. Unbeknown to her, she showed me what I lacked: the courage of my conviction to make prayer a real priority in my life. I shall always treasure our unexpected meeting. To recognise the spirit of wisdom who waits calmly and appears unexpectedly is a sure sign of God's continual presence.

The concert was a joyful experience. We sang Mozart's *Mass in C Minor* and that became a prayer for me. It was a raising of heart, mind and voice to God by allowing myself to be touched by the music and words of that inspiring composition. We may have lacked the celestial beauty of an angelic choir, but the entire experience revitalised my desire to 'pray all the time',[4] as St Paul tells us.

Such signs renew my faith that the Spirit of God is always present within us. In the Christian tradition, the Spirit signifies the love of God. It is the fulfilment of the promise Jesus made before he was arrested, tortured and crucified. He told his disciples: 'When the Spirit of truth comes he will lead you to the complete truth ... '[5]

But how can we recognise the Spirit's presence? When Jesus tried to reassure the disciples that they would not be totally bereft after his death, they were too dismayed and frightened to understand his words. We too may have been in situations where the love of God seemed absent. In the face of terrorism and natural disasters which kill, maim and disfigure thousands of people, one might well ask: 'Where is the Spirit of God? Where is God's power and love?' There are no easy answers. But I would like to suggest a possible route which may lead us to understand something of God's love at work in us and through us even at the darkest times.

I recall a true story I heard some years ago. Hans, a German-Jewish immigrant, was at a business meeting in New York. There he found himself in conversation with Max. Both men discovered that they had lived in Berlin before emigrating to the States. In the course of their conversation, Max revealed that he had been a senior officer in a concentration camp. Hans told him that he was Jewish and that several members of his family had been exterminated by the Nazis. Max seemed unmoved. He explained that he was merely working under orders and had no choice but to obey. At the end of the meeting, Hans invited Max to have dinner with him and his wife in their home the following evening. Unfortunately, Hans' wife was unwell and could not join them. However, towards the end of the evening, Hans asked her to come downstairs for a short while to meet Max. She agreed and, as she entered the room, her husband said: 'I would like you to meet our guest. He was an officer at the camp where your father was murdered.' There was a moment of stunned silence. Then she went towards Max and embraced him, saying: 'You poor man!' At this point, Max broke down and wept. The feelings he had suppressed for years were instantaneously released in his tears of remorse following an unconditional gesture of forgiveness.

For me this is a reminder that when we are touched

by unconditional love, we are in the presence of the Holy Spirit at work in us. Humanly speaking, it is impossible for many of us to be as unconditionally forgiving as this woman. But, with the support of the Spirit, the seemingly impossible can be achieved. I know this from my own experience. It is only relatively recently that I have been able to say unreservedly that I am proud of my German roots without any hidden agendas in my heart. I can give thanks for that and especially to wise friends in Germany who gently led me to this watershed in my spiritual journey.

As I look back on different stages of my life and the people who have helped me, I am filled with amazement and gratitude. But I also know that such life-giving moments are not something to be clasped or wrapped up as a personal treasure. 'You received without charge, give without charge.'[6] These words of Christ to his disciples point to the fact that the gifts we have received are not only for ourselves but they are intended to be shared as generously as they were given. It is perhaps a strange paradox that God, who gave himself freely to us, depends on us to be willing channels of the continual outpouring of his love. This, I think, lies at the heart of all our spiritual journeys.

The wisdom of God could not be in starker contrast to the wisdom of the world. Our senses are constantly bombarded with adverts promising power and material wealth. But my own experiences convince me that true and lasting happiness does not lie in that direction. God's Spirit often works through the weak and the wounded. They show us that wisdom can be attained by many different routes.

As I reflect on these events in the pilgrimage of my

life, I recall that it was a little child who, inadvertently, gave new hope to my mother. That is a delightful aspect of wisdom. It is wonderful – in the sense that it is 'full of wonder'. It can give us food for thought in our pilgrimage of life.

It was a victim of Nazi oppression who reached out to a man who had been trapped in an evil ideology. Often when we are instruments of peace to others, we are unaware of the Spirit working within us. The aspect of God's wisdom which attracts me most is that of compassion. This enables us to enter into another person's suffering and to love as unconditionally as Christ loved us.

This was also apparent in my encounter with Sister Teresa the night before I made my solemn profession. It was only in retrospect that I became aware that the Spirit of God had been present for both of us at that crucial time, helping us to respond to the power of divine wisdom within us. There have been occasions in my life when I felt that everything depended on me. I am a little wiser now.

Sometimes the gift of wisdom enables us – unbeknown to ourselves – to be silent channels of peace. The unobtrusiveness of the woman who meditated amidst the noisy chatter of our choir before our concert, is another unforgettable sign that the Spirit 'blows wherever it pleases'.[7] Often we ourselves may be unaware that wisdom is using us as its instrument or messenger.

I find it helpful to remember past events which have led me to understand that God's wisdom is at work within me. I, too, can have 'long thoughts' like trees. I think this is true for all of us. Through the awareness of such life-giving experiences we begin to recognise the power of God's love. When this happens we can take a leap into freedom and acknowledge our desire to love wisdom and follow in its footsteps.

The earth is to the sun, as the soul is to God.
The earth at any point,
Can be located by its relationship to the sun.
The earth has a scaffold of stones and trees.
In the same way a person is formed:
Flesh is the earth
The bones are the trees and stones.
The soul is the firmament of the organism, then,
in the manner in which the soul permeates the body with
its energy, it causes and consummates all human action.
This is how a person becomes a flowing orchard.
The person that does good works is indeed this orchard
bearing good fruit.
And this is just like the earth with its ornamentation of
stone and blossoming trees.[8]

EPILOGUE

TREE TALK

I am not dead, said the tree.
Don't be deceived by the
Dryness of my branches.
Look beyond the level of your eye.
There's life within.
I live out of that trust.
I am not dead, said the tree.

All my long years I have grown towards the light,
Drawn by the sun and
The mystery within the cone;
Drawn by the Son of God
That he and I fulfil our destiny.
I am not dead, said the tree.

Tip back your head, risk your balance.
Feel the firmness of the ground
Beneath your feet.
Marvel at the green-ness

EPILOGUE

Way above.
I am not dead, said the tree.

My roots are deep in eternity.
I grow beyond myself and sing
With the wind
The eternal song of love.
I shelter and listen to all
Who touch my mystery.
I am not dead, said the tree.

Sit on my roots, be still and wait.
Then you will feel the
Throbbing of life's rhythm.
Marvel at the light
On woodland carpet.
I am not dead, said the tree.

Go forth from here, trust in
Your own roots.
For you and I live for a purpose.
When you no longer see a tree,
Remember me.
I am not dead,
I am alive, said the tree.

Sr. Eva Heymann SHCJ
Glendaloch, Ireland

NOTES AND
BIBLIOGRAPHICAL
REFERENCES

Page 2

1. *The Silent Roots: Orthodox Perspectives on Christian Spirituality*,
   K. M. George, Risk Book Series (WCC Publications, Geneva,
   1994), p. 81.

Chapter 1: Christmas Trees

1. Hermann Hesse.
2. Ancient Chinese proverb, source unknown.
3. William Henry Davies, 1871–1940.
4. Revelation 21:5.
5. Hindu Prince Siddhartha Gautama, founder of Buddhism,
   563–483 BCE.

Chapter 2: Stars

1. Hermann Hesse.
2. Micah 6:8.
3. Isaiah 11:6.
4. *There Was No Path, So I Trod One: Poems*, Edwina Gateley,
   (Source Books, 1996), p. 30.

Chapter 3: Birth

1. Hermann Hesse.
2. Luke 2:15.
3. *Conamara Blues*, John O'Donohue (Doubleday, London, 2001),
   p. 65.
4. *The Mystery of Christmas*, a lecture which Edith Stein delivered

on 13 January 1931, tr. Sister Josephine Rucker (Darlington Carmel, 1985), p. 10.
5. Luke 1:38.
6. *The Mystery of Christmas*, p. 6.
7. Dr Rowan Williams, Archbishop of Canterbury, Christmas sermon 2003.

Chapter 4: When I Am Weak
1. Hermann Hesse.
2. Luke 5:4.
3. Revelation 21:5.
4. Rabindranath Tagore.

Chapter 5: Transformation
1. Hermann Hesse.
2. Psalm 46:10.
3. Ecclesiastes 3:1.
4. Psalm 139:1.
5. Isaiah 43:1.
6. The motto of Mary, Queen of Scots.
7. David Spangler, Findhorn Community.

Chapter 6: Healing Brokenness
1. Hermann Hesse.
2. Revelation 21:3, 4.
3. Albert Schweitzer.
4. John 13:38.
5. Luke 23:34.
6. *In the Heart of the Temple*, Joan D. Chittister (SPCK, 2005), p. 56.
7. *Oh God, Why?*, Gerard W. Hughes (Bible Reading Fellowship, 1993), p. 101.
8. *The Dance of Life: Spiritual Direction with Henri Nouwen*, ed. Michael Ford (Darton, Longman & Todd, 2005), p. 71.

Chapter 7: Trees Don't Talk
1. Hermann Hesse.
2. W. Goethe, quoted in *Trees*, Ansel Adams (Little, Brown & Company), p. 78.

3. Isaiah 2:3–4.
4. Druid tree lore and the Ogham.

Chapter 8: Tree Mothers
1. Hermann Hesse.
2. Jeremiah 29:11.
3. Matthew 2:13.
4. Luke 2:51.
5. *A Woman Styled Bold: The Life of Cornelia Connelly, 1809–1879*, Radegunde Flaxman (Darton, Longman & Todd, 1991), pp. 73–4.
6. *Rediscovering Mary*, Tina Beattie (Burns & Oates, 1955), p. 113.
7. John 19:26–27.
8. Deng Ming-Dao.

Chapter 9: Roots and Echoes
1. Hermann Hesse.
2. *Eternal Echoes*, John O'Donohue (Bantam, 2000), pp. 2–3.
3. *When the Trees Say Nothing*, Thomas Merton, ed. Kathleen Deignan (Sorin Books, 2003), p. 162.
4. Mark 9:22.
5. Mark 9:20–24.
6. Matthew 26:38–42.
7. *The Dance of Life*.

Chapter 10: The Wisdom of Trees
1. Hermann Hesse.
2. *You Are, Therefore I Am: A declaration of dependence,* Satish Kumar (Green Books, Devon, 2002).
3. 'The Spirit of the Beech Tree', from *The Celtic Wisdom of Trees*, Jane Gifford (Godsfield Press, 2000).
4. Ephesians 6:18
5. John 16:13.
6. Matthew 10:8.
7. John 3:8.
8. *Meditations with Hildegard of Bingen*, Gabriele Uhlein (Bear Company Inc., 1983), p. 47.